THE GREAT AWAKENING

Volume XIII

Temple Teachings from the Higher Realms

Sister Thedra

Copyright © 2021 by Halls of Light, LLC

All rights reserved. This book or any portion thereof may not be reproduced or used in any manner whatsoever without the express written permission of the publisher except for the use of brief quotations in a book review.

ISBN: 978-1-7366487-4-2

To the Reader:

This book is only a portion of the teachings and prophecies that have been given by Sananda, Sanat Kumara, and others of the Higher Realms, and Recorded by Sister Thedra.

Contents

BORACHUS 1

IN OBEDIENCE 61

PORTIONS OF THE SIBORS 135

THE SIBORS PORTIONS... 147

Mission Statement 234

Sananda's Appearance 235

Authority to Use the Name Sananda 236

About the Late Sister Thedra 238

Esu Jesus Sananda

This reproduction is from an actual photograph taken on June 1st, 1961, in Chichen Itza, Yucatan, by one of thirty archaeologists working in the area at the time. Sananda appeared in visible, tangible body and permitted His photograph to be taken.

BORACHUS

BOR: Beloved of my being- Be ye as my hand made manifest unto them and say unto them as I would say that the time draweth nigh when the door shall be closed and none shall pass; for unto the Season shall the harvest be: FOR UNTO THE SEASON SHALL THE HARVEST BE!

I SAY: ALL THINGS UNTO ITS SEASON-- There is a time / season of sowing- and a season of reaping-- and that which is sown this day shall bear fruit when the season is come.

And there shall be no greater day-- for this is the day for which ye have waited; long has this time been prophesied: when- "OLD MEN shall dream dreams- and YOUNG MEN shall have visions."

I say- young men ARE having visions, while the OLD MEN have their dreams- while they slumber and become OLD in body and weary and die---

I say- they die and perish for lack of vision: I say PITY are they: for they weary of waiting and they are not of a mind to seek out the light which is in me---

I am now prepared to bring them out of bondage, which do will to follow me-- and they which follow me shall not dream-- they shall be awakened, and they shall KNOW as I know- so be it the Fathers will that where I go they may go also. Blest art thou, I am thy Sibor and thy Brother Bor.

SORI SORI: Beloved: Behold me I come; I AM come;

I stand before thee- ever as the CHRIST- and no less- I AM the CHRIST--

I speak as such; and as such ye do receive me---

Lift up thy head--behold me in all thy day--Praise ye this day and walk which way thy crown tilts not---

Walk ye in the light of the Christ- be ye not weary of thy tasks-- I shall make light thy burden-- I shall send one unto thee- and he shall be thy servant- he shall be both hand and foot-- he shall be thy servant- while ye serve the Father-so be it and SELAH.

Behold: I AM COME: I walk with thee-- I am one with thee--I speak unto thee from out the inner temple-- I am one with thee-- I prepare a table before thee-- be ye nourished and be ye made whole--

I speak unto thee that ye may comprehend that which I say unto thee-- BEHOLD ME: I speak and ye hear me- SEE ME! and ye shall be as one with me---

Go into all the world and say unto them as I would say; that "I AM COME-- I AM WITHIN THE EARTH- as man made flesh--I come that they may know me as I am known within the realms of light---

I am light--I am SPIRIT made flesh-- Yet: my flesh binds me not-- for I am the <u>living</u> <u>SON</u> <u>of</u> <u>GOD</u>--I am ONE with the Father, and I know myself to BE-- so be it and Selah.

I come that all men may come to know as I know--I am the one which has given thee thy gift of comprehension-- Now I give unto thee the gift of sight---

Now I say ye shall see me-- and I shall touch thee and thy inner eye shall be opened--and the veil shall fall from thy eyes--I say ye shall BEHOLD ME---

For I shall come as man- and I shall speak unto thee as such and ye shall be quickened- and ye shall walk in darkness no more--be ye one which knows and KNOW that ye KNOW---

I am thy servant- thy Sibor- thy Brother the Nazarine- Jesus of Nazareth- and I am now known as Sananda Son of God---

I say I first revealed myself unto thee as such- as SANANDA I shall be known- so be it the Fathers WILL- So let it be- SELAH.

Of me shall ye be blest this day- and I shall cause thee to be filled with JOY! and GLAD shall ye be! and ye shall be blest as none other.

I am with thee and - for there is no separation one from the other -- Praise ye the name of SOLEN AUM SOLEN give unto him credit for thy being and be ye prepared for the greater part---

Sing ye praise unto Him- give thanks this day is come-- Keep it holy- and glad ye shall be -- I AM- SORI SORI.

Recorded by Sister Thedra

Moroni:

Beloved of my being: Be ye as my hand made manifest unto them and say unto them in my name, that I come into the earth as one made flesh. I come unto one called Morona- and I come as one made flesh and bone--YET, I AM SPIRIT - and of SPIRIT I shall remain-- I shall not lose my inheritance for taking embodiment through woman - it is but my part in the great hierarchal plan---

I say that many from the realm of light are now embodied--and I shall come and finish that which I began so long ago---

I say I shall finish that which I began so long ago--and I am not in the way of the world--I SHALL NOT BE! For I shall come as one which has my hand within the FATHER'S---

I shall be subject to his will- and I shall be as He would have me--- I shall not be given the bitter cup- for I have had it in ages past---

Now I speak unto thee that this may bear witness of me--and ye shall give it unto them- and they shall not deny my words--- I say: THEY SHALL NOT DENY MY WORDS--

I am now within embryo- and I shall be as none other- for I come for a certain part- and I shall finish it- so be it and SELAH.

Blest shall they be which does give me body; and care for the infant body- but I MORONI, shall not be held captive by it- I shall be different- I shall not be bound by my body--it shall serve me as need be---

I am now prepared to speak with them and they shall not be deceived---

I am Maroni (MORONI) which shall be called Maran

Recorded by Sister Thedra

The Nazarine

Beloved of my being: be ye blest of me this day; and say unto them as I would say: that there shall be mighty power released within the earth- such as they have not known---

And they shall be as ones prepared- for within the coming days they shall see the results of that which has been done through their willfulness and through their misuse of the energy which has been allotted them---

Now they shall begin the part of transmuting their part--they shall assume all responsibility of their own misused energy- that which they have mis-used-- mis-qualified and they shall be as ones blest-- They shall bless themself-- they shall be their own saviors---

They shall be as the ones responsible for all their torment and unhappiness-- and they shall be likewise responsible for their release from bondage-- for they have been bound by that which they have misused in ages past---

It is now come when the Dragon shall be disarmed-- and none shall blame HIM for their torment: for he shall be disarmed!

I say <u>they</u> shall disarm him- each shall free themself--and he shall have no power over them- so be it---

Choose this day which way ye go. I am come that ye may have light and I stand ready to bring thee out--yet ye shall not be divided against thyself - ye cannot serve two masters!

I am sent of the Father that ye may have light- that ye may be lifted up- so be it I am true unto my trust- and I am within the place of my abode prepared for to bring thee out--yet ye shall will it so--and be ye prepared to follow where I lead thee---

I am not blind- nor am I a fool- neither do I sibor fools--I am a Son of God--art thou aware of thy SON-ship? I am- and I am glad--so be it and SELAH.

I am Sananda the Nazarine

Beloved of my being: be ye blest of me and by me- I speak as one which has my hand upon thee- and I am with thee and I say unto thee I am as near as thy hand and thy foot- and I speak unto thee as myself -- I speak unto thee as one without beginning-without end- I speak unto thee from out the heart of GOD---

I speak as thy Mother Sarah- as thy parent ETERNAL- So be it that I come as such--I hold thee within my bosom and I hold thee fast- and I have kept thee for this day--and now it is come when ye shall spread thy wings as the fledgling--- And ye shall be unto thyself sufficient- ye shall be as one with me and ye shall know thyself for that which ye are and ye shall go out no more--ye shall be forever free: as ye have not remembered freedom- ye have forgotten thy days with me--and it is now come when ye shall become aware of me and ye shall turn from me no more--so be it and SELAH.

I am with thee unto the end--so be it and SELAH.

I am thy Mother Eternal Sarah.

Recorded by Sister Thedra

Sori Sori - Beloved: It is I- the Nazerine which speaks as Sori- I come as Sori Sori-- I speak as Sori Sori-- I am Sori Sori-- And be ye blest of me and by me; say unto them-- I am not bound by name- by creed- nor flesh-- I am free---

I come at will-- I speak as the Son of God and I am one with HIM- WITH HIM- I AM ONE WITH HIM, and I KNOW myself to BE- so be it and SELAH. I am at hand- and I shall not leave thee; I come that ye may be blest- so be it and Selah. I am the Nazerine.

* * *

Sori Sori- Beloved: I come unto thee this day that ye may be blest- and blest shall ye be- so be it and SELAH. I speak unto thee in tongues- many tongues have I- and I say ye shall receive the gift of tongues- and none shall confound thee---

So be it my gift unto thee-- and ye shall speak with them in their language- and ye shall be glad - so be it and SELAH.

I come that it may be so. And ye shall now say unto them which are of a mind to follow me- that I am now prepared to reveal unto them the words I have spoken at the beginning of my part unto thee--- I say when they come to understand these words they shall know me- so be it and SELAH.

I am SORI SORI; Beloved- I am with thee that ye may know me as I know thee.

SORI SORI

Recorded by Sister Thedra

Group #3 Through the Channel Rowena

I send greetings! You are all of the Inner Circle, for you have chosen the "Better part." You are not only aware of your Masters and your guides and our Lord Christ-Jesus- the Lord Immanuel- but you are seeking to obey and to live in harmony with their wishes and commands.

How few on Earth are aware or obedient! Before the end of the next decade, many more souls must reach this point. The paths of mankind diverge sharply- upward and downward- with a confused multitude milling between.

Suffering will increase, death will claim many thousands- but although your human senses will be shocked, your souls will be filled with Light and you will be radiant with Joy and vibrant with Power.

Where you are called- go quickly. Whatever you are told to do- do it without delay and perfectly. Your wills must be lost in Divine Love and Power- your minds and bodies obedient to the Heavenly Vision. As long as your earth bodies keep in vital touch with Earth life- After periods of meditation, return to your Earth duties in a spirit of Love and Service.

Avoid all criticism, or a feeling of superiority- for that, in itself, denotes weakness.

Remember to be happy in your menial duties. Learn to like what you have to do; then you will find time given to you to do what you like. As you climb the spiral stairway to Eternal Divine Light let your voices ring out in song and in laughter, as well as in prayer.

God bless you all, Your friend, Alsirian. Beloved I come this day that I might speak with thee- and that 'they' may be as ones prepared to receive me---

I say that I now prepare to come into thy presence-- and I shall walk with them as man- as one of flesh substance--- I say I shall take upon myself the body of earthly substance: and I say- that when I come it shall be for the good of all mankind--and I shall finish that which I began so long ago---

It is now come when I come as man--manifest in flesh--and I now prepare the way before me-- I say that when I come I shall be as one made flesh--- Let there be no misunderstanding about this--

ONCE IN YEARS PAST I CAME AS SPIRIT as the one from higher realms; I took not embodiment at that time--yet I WAS- and I AM- and I know myself to be—

Yet when I come I shall not be bound by flesh, for I shall not lose my freedom- I have earned that and I shall not lose it for the reason of entering into a flesh vehicle, which I shall use for the good of all mankind- for this do I come---

And it is with the consent of our Father-Mother and by HIS WILL. And the day is now come when I shall come; for the harvest is ripe- and the field is white, and I shall go forth- and walk with them- and teach them that which is now forgotten by them---

I shall be unto them their leader and I shall lead them in the way they should go---

I say I KNOW the way---I am ONE with our beloved Lord and Master SIBOR SANANDA which ye call the CHRIST- yet little do <u>they</u> know of the Christ- neither do they know the man which walks among them as Jesus Christ the beloved Nazerine, now known as Sananda--

When ye were given that name so long ago ye knew not it was thy Lord and Sibor the Nazerine whom ye adored---

I say ye knew not- and yet I say ye were first given his name- when he found thee ready to follow him-- I say ye were prepared to follow him.

Now I come for the same reason; for the reason that ye are following him-- and my words and my records shall be in good hands.

And I say ye shall be as my God-Mother-- Ye shall be as the Mother before me-- Ye shall be as my hand made manifest while I wait maturity of body---

I say ye shall receive me in SPIRIT- while the youth takes maturity- and the work shall be accomplished- and it shall be done according to the will of God the Father Mother.

I am now prepared to speak unto them which are of a mind to learn and I say they shall profit to hear me- and to heed that which I say-- I say I come forth to finish that which I began many years ago- and it IS SO- and SO BE IT; IT SHALL BE DONE. I am thy Sibor and thy Brother MARONI.

Recorded by Sister Thedra

Thedra speaking:

For a greater understanding of these records see the history of Joseph Smith-to refer to a more recent record; for it is this work that our beloved Sibor refers to "which was begun so long ago." The male parent-to-be has been brought to me for certain work over a year ago- Maroni has been speaking to him-- and also the young mother-to-be.

Maroni says "I came as Spirit" (to Joseph Smith).

Sori Sori: Blest of me shall ye be this day - go into all the world and proclaim me: and say unto them in my name- I am come- and I speak unto them as man---

And I say: I AM COME-- I am within the body of flesh, as man-- yet my body binds me not! I say; "I AM HERE" - and I shall go unto any whosoever which prepares himself to receive me---

I say; I shall go unto any one; which so ever prepares himself for to receive me---

He shall be as one un-opinionated- he shall be as one which has no malice in his heart-- he shall be as one which has a mind to receive me.

He shall be as one made GLAD! for I come that they may have light---

I bring unto thee great light; and when it is come that ye are prepared to receive me ye shall be strong enough to endure my light---

I say: I shall not lower my light for thy sake-- it was once done; and forever---

I say ye have gone this way before and ye shall now be as one free from the wheel of rebirth, when ye prepare thyself to receive me for I am come that ye may be free.

I say it shall be finished this day- so be it and SELAH.

I am thy Brother the Nazerine which trod the self-same path so long ago -- now ye shall be as I am - and whither I goest ye shall go- so be it and Selah.

I am thy Sibor and thy Brother; Bless thee that ye have received me, and I shall speak with thee that they may have the next part for them which have asked- so be it and SELAH. I am Sananda.

Sori Sori: Beloved of my being: this day I greet thee with open arms stretched forth that ye may come to me into my place of abode---

And I would say unto thee this day ye have prepared thyself well-- I say ye have been faithful in all things- ye have kept the faith when thy trials have been hard to bear.

I say ye have held fast when the tempest stormed about thee- and great has been thy trials- yet greater still shall be thy reward--for have I not said. so? And so be it---

I am he which came unto thee upon the road side so long ago; to whom ye offered food and drink, while they babbled as fools: I say they knew me not: neither did they proffer me food---

I say none save thee proffered me food and drink-- NONE!

I say they would have rushed to give unto me their puny food had they recognized me- yet I say; I need not their food- for I am one with my source- and I do not need earth's substance to feed my body-- I am not a slave unto it-- it binds me not- and I am not bound by anything- neither am I of the Netherworld---

I say I am not bound by creeds nor dogmas--nor by flesh! Nor by laws of earth-- neither does my Father limit me--- I am free-- I am boundless-- I go where I will- and I come unto thee that ye too may know such freedom---

I am now prepared to receive thee as thou art prepared to come-- I am with thee unto the end- so be it and SELAH. I am Sori Sori- Sananda the Nazerine so be it ye shall give this unto them and they shall bear witness of these my words; and they shall go on record- that thy records may be complete, for it has not yet become apparent that which ye shall be given to do. I am thy Sibor and thy Brother Sananda Son of God the Father.

Recorded by Sister Thedra

Beloved: I am come that ye may be blest- so be it and Selah. I speak with thee as one with thee- there is no separation with us-- Ye have found thy way- and I am glad - I have come unto thee for that purpose- yet- MY BELOVED; I say unto thee- it is now come when I shall walk with thee, side by side; and I shall counsel thee in thy new part, so be it and Selah.

Now ye shall be as my hand made manifest upon the earth- ye shall speak unto them as I would speak--I shall invest within thee the power and the authority befitting a SON of GOD, and ye shall walk accordingly- ye shall bless them as I bless thee- ye shall bless them as I would; ye shall be unto them the hand of God the Father; ye shall be unto them all HE would have thee be.

Ye shall walk with head high- thy mind staid on HIM, and HIS WILL for thee; ye shall NOT be part of them and their foolishness; for ye shall be separate from them: Ye shall bless them and be a lamp unto their feet; and ye shall go into all the world as my feet and as my hands- and ye shall declare unto them that I AM COME-I AM COME!

And ye shall be as the VOICE of God- the Father Mother-- ye shall be as one in authority for ye shall know that which ye say; ye shall go out as one prepared; and ye shall bear the SEAL of SOLOMON upon thy forehead.

And ye shall weary not- nor shall ye faint. I say ye shall faint not nor shall ye be in want; for I shall be unto thee all that ye have need of.

I shall be unto thee thy hand and thy feet--I shall be unto thee thy mouth--

I shall put words into it; and they shall GLORIFY the FATHER which gave unto thee being---

I am with thee unto the end- I am Sananda the Nazerine.

Beloved: I come that ye may be blest- and so shall ye-- I say unto thee ye have questioned- IF - the foregoing part shall go out unto them: I say YES! and it shall profit them to receive these MY WORDS, for they shall bear witness of these MY WORDS--and it has not become apparent that which shall be given unto thee to do---

I say ye shall be as one which has gone the long way to bless them; and ye shall be as one in authority, and ye shall be as one which has the power which the Father has willed unto thee-- ye shall be his hand maiden- his servant- and for this have ye been prepared.

I say that this is a school of which they know little; yet it is My part to bring this school into the outer world- wherein they may find themself.

I say when MOHAMET does not- or can not- go to the Mountain- we bring the MOUNTAIN unto MOHAMET---was that expected of me?

I am now in my place of abode prepared to bring into outer manifestation the great MYSTERY SCHOOL- which has been spoken of so often - wherein they labor for years- for such as I am now giving unto thee.

I say; that they which do apply themself and have a will to learn and which are trust worthy- shall now - THIS DAY, be prepared for the GREATER PART: they shall no longer go into the far places; but in the confines of their dwelling places shall they prepare themself.

And as they receive these MY WORDS- these MY MESSENGERS; MY SERVANTS; so do they receive me--and when they receive me I shall come in and Sibor them: and I say; for this shall they prepare themself- and I shall not be fooled--

I say unto them; DECEIVE NOT THYSELF- FOR YE ALONE ARE ACCOUNTABLE FOR ALL THY FOOLISHNESS- THY MISUSED ENERGY: AND ALL THY TORMENT.

I say; THIS DAY YE SHALL BEGIN ANEW!

And transmute all thy misused energy - all thy misqualified substance; and ye shall be as one wise to cleanse thyself; and I say unto thee: LOVE YE ONE ANOTHER: I AM WITH THEE IN FLESH AND BONE: AND I SPEAK AS MAN: AND I SHALL COME UNTO THEE WHEN YE ARE PREPARED TO RECEIVE ME- I AM THE WAYSHOWER- NOW KNOWN AS SANANDA SON OF GOD.

Recorded by Sister Thedra

Beloved; I come as thy guardian; and as thy brother; I am Borachus, I speak unto thee as such; I AM THY BROTHER; and thy Sibor; and I give unto thee one commandment; BE YE ALERT! FOR THERE IS ONE WHICH SHALL COME UNTO THEE IN SHEEPS CLOTHING-- and he shall be as one with an OFFERING in his hand; and ye shall be as one wise to refuse it; for he shall be as one with TWO FACES---

One facing the NORTH- one facing the SOUTH; while he SAYS- he is traveling EAST; I SAY: HE IS NOT! Yet I say unto thee-- HE HAS TWO FACES: and he has them BOTH OUT! For them which are yet unwise: I say he shall betray his hand; and he shall be as one exposed at his own game so be it and Selah.

I say ye shall know him for that which he is; now ye shall give unto him this word: and ye shall remember this:- THAT HE SHALL TRY TO DECEIVE THEE: AND HE SHALL SPIT WORDS OF HONEY FROM HIS TONGUE: AND HE SHALL BE AS ONE FILLED WITH

DECEIT--AND HE SHALL BETRAY HIMSELF; so be it and SELAH.

I am thy Sibor and thy Guardian, Borachus.

Sori Sori: Beloved I say it is so- and so it is; and ye shall remember this; THAT THEY WHICH WOULD TRY TO DECEIVE ME IS THE GREATEST OF FOOLS: SO BE IT AND SELAH. I AM THY SIBOR, Sananda.

Recorded by Sister Thedra

By My Grace

Beloved of my being; By my grace shall ye be brought out of bondage. And I am with thee this day that it may be so- so be it and SELAH. I come that ye this day, be brought out; and I say ye shall be; so be it and SELAH.

I am now prepared to bring thee into the place where in I am- and I say ye have prepared thyself for to receive so be it that ye shall be as one rewarded for thy efforts: I say great shall be thy reward and it is SO! I say so and SO it is.

I am now giving unto thee my gift of seeing and hearing - and yes shall see as I see, and hear as I hear and ye shall be glad- so be it and SELAH.

I speak and ye hear me: I stand before thee and ye see me; and I shall sit with thee and consul thee - and I shall give unto thee many gifts which have been kept for thee so be it the Fathers will; I say; ye shall have that which has been kept for thee- so be it the Fathers will- I am with thee that this may be accomplished this day- I say it shall be.

Blest art thou- and blest shall ye be- I say ye shall be blest---

I am now prepared to speak unto them which are as yet in bondage and they shall bear witness of these my words unto thee- and they shall be caused to remember them, and they shall profit there by.

I am now prepared to walk among them; and I shall seek out them which are prepared to receive me. I am now prepared to go unto them where ever they be; there is no hiding place-- and I am not blind -- I say I shall find them and they shall be made to see and hear and to know---

I am now come that they may be found - and that they may be brought in, and prepared for the greater part--- Was I not sent of the Father that this day may bear fruit? And I say the harvest is now ready- and the field is white; so be it that I come to find my own - and I weary not --neither shall I return into HIM until I have found them and delivered them up.

Pity are they which deny me for I come for their sake- and for their own benefit do I come into the world of man as one of flesh and bone. I say; I COME AS ONE OF FLESH AN BONE- THAT THEY MAY KNOW ME--- I say, I COME TO BRING THEM OUT --YET- THEY SHALL CHOOSE TO FOLLOW ME.

And yet they are to be found in the dens of the Dragon- and they ask NOT of me!

Yet some shall awaken- and they shall be unveiled and do mighty works ere the end cometh; I say none shall be overlooked- nor neglected for I am not about to betray myself nor my trust--so be it that I shall send out my emissaries and I shall give unto them the power and the authority to speak for me; and I shall endow them with the gift of speech and they shall say that which I shall give unto them to say-- and they shall be my mouth - MY VOICE- made manifest unto them---

And when they have accepted these my words- my emissaries- MY SERVANTS, I shall make myself known unto them ; and I shall come in and consul them - and I shall reveal unto them many things which shall profit them, and they shall be glad!

I am thy Sibor and thy Brother. The Nazerine Sananda- Jesus Christ

Recorded by Sister Thedra

Beloved I come unto thee this day that ye may be blest; and I say unto thee that ye shall be blest so be it and SELAH.

I say ye shall have thy head unbound- and ye shall know as I know- and ye shall be glad for thy knowing so be it and SELAH---

I say ye shall be free even as I am free: I say: ye shall have thy memory restored unto thee and ye shall be eternally glad- so be it and SELAH.

I am now prepared to bring them in which are prepared to receive me and of me -- I say unto them: which are yet in bondage- BE YE ALL MIND TO RECEIVE ME AND OF ME: AND I SHALL FIND

THEE AND I SHALL BRING THEE INTO THE PLACE WHEREIN I AM AND YE SHALL BE GLAD FOREVER MORE.

I shall repeat: YE SHALL FIRST PREPARE THYSELF FOR TO RECEIVE ME—YE SHALL BE OF A MIND TO LEARN: AND WHEN YE HAVE RECEIVED MY MESSENGERS/MY EMISSARIES AND MY SERVANTS IN MY NAME AND WHEN YE HAVE ENGRAVEN UPON THY HEART THESE MY WORDS. I SHALL COME UNTO THEE AND SIBOR THEEIN THE WAY OF THE WISE: SO BE IT AND SELAH.

I say ye shall be as ones blest of me and by me; for I shall touch thee and ye shall be made whole- so be it and SELAH.

I am thy Brother which is known as The Wayshower, and I have been called by many names; yet they which proclaim me by name- and follow me not are the un-KNOWING ones; they KNOW ME NOT!

Such is my word unto them this day-- I am Sananda / Jesus The Nazerine, born of Mary, - the ward of Joseph--Now within the realms of light wherein ye shall be brought: all which do the Fathers will and who do choose to follow me---

I say unto thee be ye not deceived for NOT ALL which do say: "LORD LORD" know me; they delude themself - they are as ones deceived---

I say: I am not deceived- for I know them; and I am forever watchful of my own-- I see them - and I draw nigh unto them---

I speak unto them- and I give unto them of my grace that they may endure-- and I say; endure <u>they shall</u>! For I shall not forsake them- and

I shall bless them- and they shall be caught up with me- and where I go they shall go---

Yet I say; THEY TEMPT ME NOT! For I am not deceived! I see- and know that which motivated their action--- I say they are as the wayward children which know not the law--- Them, which guard and keep the records--they know---

And they which would deceive themself are the traitors unto <u>themselves</u>- they are fearful of little things; they run hither and yon - and they seek the light in far places--when they have but to be still- and and know that I AM NEARER THAN HAND AND FOOT-- THAT I KNOW THEM EVEN BEFORE THEY HAVE SPOKEN--- I say they shall AWAKEN!

And they shall now stir- and go into ACTION! AND PROVE themself: and then I shall reveal myself unto them---

I say: THIS IS THE DAY OF ACTION-WHEN THEY SHALL BE AS ADULTS! WHEN THEY SHALL TURN FROM THEIR CHILDISH WAYS: AND WHEN THEY SHALL ABIDE IN ME: AND WITHIN THE LAWS SET FORTH WITHIN THESE SCRIPTS---

So be it that I am now prepared to to reveal great things unto them which have mystified them.

I say they have walked in darkness- and now it shall end and they shall be brought out forever; they shall be freed from the wheel of re-birth - and they shall walk with me KNOWINGLY---

I say the path I walk is short- safe -and LIGHT: One born of GOD, am I, and beside HIM there is none other: I AM and I know- I AM- and where I go I shall take thee and ye shall be glad forever more- so be it and SELAH. I am SANANDA.

Recorded by Sister Thedra

Beloved, faithful ones; ye have come to this altar as called and ye shall be greatly blest. This is the time of the full moon when the vibrations are higher than at other times - greater strength and help has poured out to thee during this time and ye have felt the strong vibrations and have not been able to relax fully.

All help possible is given to the children who are walking as led in the path of light which leads to the FATHER'S house, and freedom from all bondage such as ye are laboring under on this sorrowful plane.

Be ye ever faithful and ye will be led into peace that passeth all understanding and ye will be sorrowful no more.

My peace I give unto thee, I am thy Older Brother, SANANDA.

Recorded by SOREA SOREA

Blessings to all; May you let love pour forth; love born of compassion for all men and GOD. Let this Divine Love pour forth with all thoughts; when you wish to be critical pour forth a prayer of Divine Love instead. Ask your Father Mother God to aid you in this pouring forth of love;

for only Divine Love born of Divine compassion can truly protect you and help you in your growth.

I am happy that I have been granted the permission to speak to you of this DIVINE LOVE. SELAH and PEACE BE WITH YOU. Guatma Buddha,

Recorded by Jo Ann

Beloved of my being; I bless thee this day, and I speak unto thee for the good of all mankind- and I say, ye shall give unto them these words and they which do receive them shall be blest; so be it and SELAH.

I am thy Sibor Sananda, which has gone before thee to prepare the way before thee--and ye have received unto thyself these my words- and my plan-- and ye have been unto me a faithful hand servant; and I shall bless thee; and I shall be unto thee all that ye shall need; so be it and SELAH.

I am now come that ye may be brought out of bondage; that thy days of un-KNOWING may be ended; so be it and SELAH.

I bring unto thee a plan and ye shall be as one which has proven thyself worthy to receive it in its fullness- so be it and Selah.

I am now prepared to come unto thee which has served me well; and to give unto thee the greater plan-- I am within my place of abode for that purpose- so be it and Selah. I am thy Sibor Sananda, Go in PEACE and prepare; for this day shall bear fruit, so be it and Selah.

I am thy servant--Sananda.

Sori Sori; Beloved; I greet thee this day as one mindful of thy SPIRIT and of thy limitations; and I say unto thee that ye shall be as one brought into the place where in I am and ye shall be as one blest-

I say ye shall not be bound by <u>them</u> which have not grown into ADULTHOOD: I say they shall be <u>responsible</u> for themself; and they shall carry the burden for themself; I say they can burden themself- and they shall not place it upon thy shoulders.

I am now prepared to give unto thee that which I have kept for thee- and I am now in the place where in I am prepared to bring <u>them</u> in- and they shall prepare themself to come; I say they shall be blest of me and by me, so be it and Selah.

I am thy Sibor and I have sibored thee <u>well</u>; I am thy brother which has gone before thee to prepare the way before thee, and I say ye have received me unto thyself - and ye have obeyed every commandment and ye have been as my hand made manifest unto them---

Now ye shall walk among them as one in authority and as one prepared. I say ye shall be as one in authority- and ye shall be as my mouth-- I shall be give unto thee the part which I have kept for thee and ye shall be glad- so be it and SELAH, I am thy Sibor Sananda.

Recorded by Sister Thedra

Beloved: I say unto thee- this day ye shall be unto me my hands made manifest unto them which gather themself together for the purpose of learning.

I say they have gathered themself together many times; yet they know me not-- for I am the unknowable- <u>until</u> they have walked and talked with me: and become <u>AS</u> <u>I</u> <u>AM</u>: then they shall KNOW me.

And <u>then</u> they shall do the things which I do-- and they shall do the things which they NOW talk about---

There shall be NO more Mysteries- No more hidden secrets- for <u>ALL</u> things shall be revealed unto them which come into the place wherein I AM---

I say-- they shall know as I know--and there is nothing hidden from me- for I AM and I know I AM ONE with the Father Mother God.

Now: say unto them in my name--that I am among them in flesh and bone--and I shall be unto them the Fathers hand made flesh: for I shall come in HIS NAME- and I shall be as HIS VOICE--and I shall say that which HE gives me to say-- for I shall be unto myself true- and I shall neither betray myself nor my trust---

So be it that I AM the Father made flesh; and I know that I am a SON of GOD - known as SANANDA, and I shall walk accordingly---

I am thy hand-- I speak and ye hear me- and ye give of thyself that they may be blest-- and I now send thee forth- that they might have these my words; that they may be prepared for to receive me---

I shall go forth unto ALL the world in due time; yet- I walk now among them in the way of the INITIATE that they may be prepared for the GREAT DAY when I shall make my grand appearance---

I say; I shall come as a thief in the night-- when they least expect me-- I say they have waited long for me; yet now that I am here they believe me not!

I say many shall be caught napping; and they shall be as the ones which have thrown overboard their own life belts---

I say they shall be as the ones which betray themself --

I say they have not heard that which I say---

I AM HERE---

I am within the world of men; as MAN MADE FLESH---

I say that HE- which hear me shall accept unto himself these my words, and unto <u>HIM</u> shall I give the gift of comprehension--I speak unto <u>them</u> which have ears to hear-- and I give not of my jewels unto babes which know not their value--I am not so foolish as to waste my energy--- I say- I sibor NOT fools---

I come that this day may bear fruit; and all WHOSOEVER accepts these my words unto themself and engrave them upon their heart- HIM shall I seek out---

I say I am not an imposter--I go not where I am not invited-- I say - I go not into dark places; and I fear NAUGHT- for I am of the

FATHER SENT- so be it nothing can touch me-- for I am all powerful-- all KNOWING---

And NEVER AGAIN shall I lower MY LIGHT--I say- I shall NOT EVER AGAIN be 'the crucified one'--- NEVER AGAIN shall they martyr men which has been sent of GOD---

I say the day of MARTYRDOM is past and none shall be part of such diabolic practice; for this is the NEW AGE--the age of light- when all men shall turn unto the light yet- unto the day- each unto his own-- the harvest is longer for some- and shorter for others-- I say--THE WHEAT SHALL NOT BEAR THISTLES: NOR THE ACORN BECOME THE BERRY-- for I say that each unto his own---

And I shall not be deceived; for I shall know them <u>as they are</u>-- I shall find them by <u>their own</u> <u>light</u> and when it is sufficient I shall come in and I shall walk and talk with them---

Yet they- and THEY ALONE- shall prepare themself---

I bring unto thee the laws; and I say unto thee- LOVE covers them ALL-- and in TRUTH and REALITY there is but the Law of LOVE.

And I now come that ye may know the foolishness of preaching the law of VICARIOUS ATONEMENT

And I say that <u>they</u> <u>alone</u> shall be responsible for all their unseeming deeds- all their mis-used energy which has been sent out pure and unadulterated - and they shall purify and make clean ALL their THOUGHTS-- ALL their WORDS- which <u>create</u> like unto them-

I say - they cry- for DELIVERANCE! FROM WHAT?

27

WHEN THEY BIND THEMSELF BY EVERY WORD WHICH PROCEEDS FROM OUT THEIR MOUTH?

I say-- they either loosen themself from bondage- or they bind themself: for I am as one which sees and knows--

I see them bound fast by that which they weave for themself -- they design- fashion for themself their own bounds---

They use the WORD of GOD for their own end-- they speak that which is not prompted by love-- and they speak as ones with a venomous tongue-- and they are as ones with spurious words---

They speak deceitfully - they are hypocrites- and blasphemers---

I say: <u>they</u> say-- "LORD LORD" --- and they know me not!

I say: they speak of and about me yet they abide not by that which I say-- they hear me not!

And neither have they the WILL nor strength of character.

NOW- I speak unto THEM- WHO ASK OF ME - and have the MIND to LEARN- and the WILL to follow me:-

I say unto thee: that; they shall follow where I lead- and they shall go the ROYAL ROAD- and they shall be caught up with me-- and they shall not taste of death.

I say; THEY SHALL NOT DIE---

I say; that- they shall be forever free of the wheel of rebirth- and they shall go into darkness no more---

Neither shall they languish in the field for the pittance of bread.

I say they shall be free-born-- born of God the Father, and they shall NOT die---

Neither shall they be born of womb- of woman-- I say they shall be forever free of the wheel of rebirth---

NOW- I speak unto them which have given of themself that others may be lifted up; they shall be as the EMISSARIES of GOD the Father- they shall walk among them as ones worthy to be called "EMISSARY"- they shall receive their inheritance in full-- they shall be rewarded in like measure---

I say-- they shall know their FATHER, which has given unto them being-- I say - that they shall <u>BECOME</u> SONS of GOD: Now ye shall walk as I point; thy feet shall not stray- neither shall they trip over little things---

I say- they shall be planted firmly upon the path of TRUTH; and LIGHT--and they shall neither go to the right nor to the left--but <u>firmly</u> straight ahead---

My way - is the STRAIGHT and SAFE one: I say none shall find the pits wherein they may be trapped; when they follow me; for I come that they may be delivered out---

I say - STRAIGHT and LIGHT -- SAFE and SURE is my way---

Yet I speak unto thee My Beloved ONES:

Many are the ANTI-CHRISTS which move among thee---

And ye which do work in my vineyard shall know them by their fruits; for they shall be as my servants; and ye shall be as a thorn in their shoes; yet, ye shall know them for that which they are--and they shall be afraid!

And they shall be tormented by their own doing- and by that which they send out- which shall rebound upon them, and they shall be tormented--GREAT TORMENT shall they know---

I say- it shall be their cross- and heavy shall it be!

I say, the ANTI-CHRISTS shall be as ones which shall pass, as the chaff in the wind!

For I speak a TRUTH- and I know of which I speak---

I say unto thee--THEIR DAY IS COME WHEN THEY SHALL BE AS THE WORD WHICH HAS GONE OUT FROM THEM---

They shall be removed and put into the places prepared for them wherein they shall wait for a NEW Day- wherein they shall be brought to maturity. I said: "EVERYTHING ACCORDING TO ITS SEASON"--so be it according unto law-- and it is so--and so it shall be.

I bless thee MY Servant; my hand made manifest; now I command thee "GO UNTO THEM IN MY NAME" and I shall bless thee--and I shall likewise bless them which do receive my servant in whom I am well pleased--so be it I shall put my words into thy mouth---

And I shall give unto thee fresh new energy - and I shall abide within thee---

Go in Peace- and LOVE them in my name. I am Sananda, known unto them as Jesus Christ, born of Mary, ward of Joseph, (The Nazerine).

(Given to Sister Thedra for the convention at Triumph, Idaho)

Sori Sori: I speak unto thee my beloved; and thou hast heard me: I say unto thee. "BE AT PEACE THIS DAY-AND YE SHALL BE BLEST". For I am with thee--and I am at thy hand--and I am not to forsake thee--for have I not been unto thee sufficient?

I say that I am now prepared to give unto them a plan by which they are to work- and use for the good of all man-kind: I say they shall work and bring about their own deliverance FIRST- and THEN they shall be as ones prepared for the GREATER PART--

THEN - and ONLY then can they deliver others: I say they shall put from them their "puny ways"- their <u>childishness</u>: and they shall be as ones PATIENT and <u>willing</u> for me to lead the way---

I say; "THEY SHALL BE PATIENT" and <u>WILLING</u> FOR ME TO LEAD THE WAY.

They shall FIRST- learn their own lessons; for this is the day of preparation; and then the DAY OF ACTION- FIRST: PREPARATION--THEN ACTION!

Now let this be recorded that--the ACTION follows the preparation---

Was I not prepared for my part? And have I not been better for it?

I say- I have prepared myself --that I might serve the Father's plan. I say- I AM ACTION- "LOVE IN ACTION"-- and I am not in lethargy--I am not asleep!

And I say unto thee: be ye not silent upon their willfulness--nor upon their waywardness; for I am not!

I speak fearlessly- and I am not bound by the law of man; neither do I bid for favors--I ask of them NAUGHT--but obedience unto the law---

Now say unto them in MY NAME that I am not of a mind to Sibor the foolish- nor the willful--for I have given unto them much which should benefit them---

And I am not of a mind to soothe their little wounds! I say they shall lick them themself---

For I have said: "I send out my servants in MY NAME- and they have not been mindful of them--they have not received them as they would ME" –

I say: "AS THEY WOULD ME."

Now ye shall say- as I would: that the privilege of giving is as glorious as to receive---

And I say they ask to receive; yet they have not the mind to comprehend the LAW of giving--and as surely- as the night follows the day the reward follows (the giving) and in like measure.

I bear witness unto this; and as they give grudgingly the likeness follows also--I say the return of their grudging is exact: I say as they send out-so does the reward return in likeness.

Now ye shall add that: wherein have I given another the AUTHORITY to be called the "TEMPLE OF SANANDA SANAT KUMARA"?

None other have I ordained as such---

I say I have ordained this Temple: I have inhabited this TEMPLE: I have spoken in this TEMPLE: I have stood upon this altar; and I have spoken that YE may have these my words--that YE may bear witness of them---

And I say- they which have given grudgingly shall be as ones which shall learn the lesson of giving--I say they shall be as ones which have been brought face to face with their own foolishness---

For I say--they have been unmindful of my servant- they have given credit unto the others which I have not authorized as a servant--and were- and are not- MY VASSALS----

I say I am mindful of all my sheep--I hear their call and I send one of my servants to bring them in- and when it is brought in and fed - should it not eat- and if it should choose to die-- it is not of my account; for I am forever mindful of their cry! And none is overlooked- nor forgotten---

I say I sent my servant into the places where in they were lamenting--and asking for help and they were given what was necessary--yet they were as ones which had their fingers in their ears, and their hands before their eyes- and they see not--neither do they hear my words!

I say: THEY HEAR <u>NOT</u> WHAT I SAY! They prattle on as fools. I say: I do not give of my pearls unto babes who know not their worth.

I am ever mindful of their efforts- and for such are they better; yet, why have they not given unto my servant- as they would unto me?

I am the Master in this TEMPLE; THE PRIEST; why give unto the one at the gate which has yet not entered?

I say: they as yet have not entered within the gate- and they shall be as ones prepared--so be it none other shall enter therein.

I am not of a mind to preach--yet it shall be recorded that I KNOW them- and that which goes on!

I say I am not so minded to give unto them my gems; my jewels without price--

I say they shall EARN them; and too- I say the price is not a few trinkets; nor is it of earthly substance--I say I am not so foolish as to ask of them PENNIES; yet they shall bear the burden of the work which I give unto my servant--for they too profit there by---

I am not about to carry them on my back--neither shall I ask of my servant that she shall carry them on hers.

I say - they shall be responsible for their part- so be it I have spoken - and it is recorded as spoken; I shall command it be given in like manner and they shall bear witness of this-MY WORD. I am Sananda.

Christ Speaketh: "The Word"

Sori Sori:

Beloved I speak unto thee this day for the good of all mankind, So let it be. I AM now prepared to speak unto them which have asked that I speak---

I say that I AM come that they may have Light; and that they may know me. I AM not afar- neither am I of the netherworld. I say, I AM as near as hand and foot- I AM with thee- I say,

I AM with thee- and I know thee as I know myself ---

I speak in language which ye comprehend - yet, I speak in any language for I AM language - I AM The Word- I cause The Word to be- I AM the cause of The Word- I create The Word- I AM all that I create- and I create wisely- I create like unto the Father Mother God.

I AM the Father made manifest among men- I AM He which was and is the Son of God, sent forth that ye may be brought out of bondage. I say, I AM sent of the Father Mother God that the ye may return unto Him this day- I AM in flesh and bone for this purpose.

Yet I go not into the places of iniquity wherein they pour forth and I speak wisely, for I know that which I say- They live for the pleasure of the senses, and they ask not of nor for my counsel---

I say, I AM not of a mind to enter into their dens of iniquity; I go not into the dark places- for I AM no part of them- yet as they seek me out I go the long way to find them.

I AM with thee that ye may do my work- and that ye too may follow in my foot-steps, that where I go ye may go also- I shall lead the way and ye shall walk with dignity and surety.

I bless thee this day- and I go with thee every mile of the way and I shall bless them which receive my words- I say unto thee: "Hail! Hail! I AM Come! I AM Come! Bless This Day and Keep It Holy!"

I AM with thee- and I shall abide with thee until it is finished. I bless thee- and I say unto thee, all who seek me out shall find me, and I shall come in and speak with thee.

I AM The Nazerine, born of Mary- The Ward of Joseph---

So Be It; So Be It Is Selah..

Recorded by Sister Thedra

Beloved of my being: I greet this day in the name of our adorable Father Mother God; unto him all praise and glory. I speak with thee that ye may know as I know. I come that ye may have thy head unbound -- that ye may be free even as I am free, I speak with thee that ye may know that there is no separation in the realm of Spirit and Love -- one within the Father Mother God are we -- no separation.

I say I give unto thee a part and others give unto thee a part, and yet there is only One -- many have fragments of the whole and ye have the laws governing the whole -- or: which is contained within the whole. LOVE covers the laws -- and all that has or ever shall be written is covered within these scripts. There are many variations, many wordy discourses written on and about the law. Yet I say the Law of Love covers all that shall ever be written concerning thy freedom.

I say that thy freedom is assured thee when ye love as I love. And I say that when ye love as I love ye shall be as I am, and when the time is come that ye can lift the dead, heal the sick, and restore the sight unto the blind, ye are as the "physician" -- and until ye can do this ye are not the "physician" -- neither art thou master.

I say I am the Sibor, ye are the Sibet, the fledgling. And I am now prepared to bring thee out of bondage and give unto thee as I have received. So be it and Selah. I am with thee unto the end. I am Sananda.

Borich speaking and I bring into thee greetings from the light realms. I speak unto thee as thy brother. I say unto thee ye shall be as one prepared for the greater part. And it is my part to guide and guard thee from harm and to be thy hand servant. I say I shall be with thee by day and by night. And I say I shall be at thy service and ye shall be as one blest. So be it and Selah. I am thy servant and thy brother, Borich.

Sori - Beloved I speak unto thee as the Christ. I speak unto thee in thy own language. Yet language is no object to me -- no obstacle -- no barrier. I am free from all barriers, all obstacles. I speak unto thee for thy own sake: Ye shall be as one free from all the work which consumes thy time.

I say that which shall be given unto thee to do shall consume thy time. Ye shall be as one blest and ye shall have no other to consume thy energies, for I say one shall be sent unto thee and he shall be unto thee thy hand and thy foot. He shall be unto thee that which I would have him be and I say he shall be unto thee all that I would have him be. I am now prepared to bring him. So be it and Selah.

I am thy son and thy sibor, Sananda

Recorded by Sister Thedra

Beloved of my being. Be ye blest of me and by me, for this am I come. I say unto thee ye have sat with me and ye have counseled with me, and by my hand have ye been led. I say ye have counseled with me, and I say unto thee I have touched thy hand with mine and I have spoken with thee and ye have answered me. I say ye have answered me. And when I walked the shores of Galilee ye trod the selfsame shore. Ye brought unto me food and drink.

And ye sat with me in the upper room for the purpose of counseling and for the purpose of preparing thyself for this day. Yet ye knew not that I should not return for so long. I say ye knew not the time I would be away. I am now returned to keep my promise, for I said I should return. Now ye shall be as one prepared to receive me, and ye shall be glad. So be it and Selah. I am Sananda.

(Thedra: Are you speaking unto the two of us? Yes: ye both were as sisters -- one in spirit -- yet two individuals, with one purpose of mind. Sananda.)

Beloved of my being: I say unto thee it is now come when ye shall go out as my hand, as my feet, and ye shall touch them and they shall be filled with the Holy Ghost.

They shall be filled with the "Spirit of God," for I shall endow thee with the gift of healing. Ye shall heal their infirmities. Ye shall be unto them all the Father would have thee be, and ye shall bless them in his name. I say ye shall bless them in his name.

Now I say ye shall be unto them all the Father would have thee be. I say ye shall bless them as I would bless them. So be it and Selah. I am thy son and thy sibor, Sananda.

Recorded by Sister Thedra

Beloved of my being: Blest are thou this day and blest shall ye be. I say ye shall be blest this day and ye shall go into the place wherein they lie dying and stinking; and ye shall heal them in my name and ye shall lift them up. And they shall walk and they shall be made to leap with joy. And they shall go out and bless others as they have been blest. So be it and Selah.

I say they shall be blest as I have been blest and they shall be mindful of that which has been done for them. So be it and Selah. I say they shall be blest and they shall be mindful of their benefactors. So be it the better part of wisdom. I say when they are healed they shall remember from whence their blessings came. Be ye as one prepared for thy new part.

I say ye shall go out into the world of man as one prepared to heal them -- and ye shall lift them up in my name. And ye shall heal them and they shall be blest of me through thee. And they shall be filled with joy. And they shall leap up for joy and they shall remember their blessings. And I say they shall be blest -- and they shall remember from whence it came.

I have spoken and ye have recorded these my words. Now ye shall give them unto the ones who have asked for them. So be it they shall profit thereby. I am thy sibor and thy older brother. I am the sibor of sibors. I am the physician of physicians. I say ye shall heal them in my name and none shall touch thee. None shall lay hands upon thee. None shall be unto thee a power of authority. For I say there is no higher authority, and I shall send thee forth as my hand and as my mouth and none shall impede thy progress nor torment thee, for I say I shall be unto thee all that ye shall need. I shall be unto thee all which ye need.

I shall send forth my servants to serve thee and they shall be loyal unto me. I say they shall be loyal unto me. They shall be true unto me and unto themself, and unto their trust. I say they shall serve me as they serve thee, for they which serve the Father serve me and they which serve my servants also serve the Father and me. So be it and Selah. I am thy sibor, Sananda.

Recorded by Sister Thedra

At the Altar --

Father Mother God, I come on behalf of this my beloved sister. What would you say to her through this hand?

Sori Sori -- I come my beloved in answer to thy call. I am he which has been sent of God the Father that thy call be answered. I say unto thee that no call which is prompted by love shall go unheard, unanswered. So be it I come in love that thy answer be given thee. So be it for the good of all mankind. I say unto thee I am within hearing. I am not afar off. I am with thee; there is no hiding place. I know thee and I am not afraid to speak unto thee.

When ye are so prepared I shall come in and counsel thee and I shall speak in language which ye can comprehend. I say ye shall know that which I say unto thee for I speak simply and I am not deceived by flowery speech. I need no better words than ye use unto thy other friends. Speak unto me as ye would unto them and I can understand thee. I am not a moody man.

I am at all times ready to hear thy words and I ask of thee nothing more than to be unto thyself true, and I shall do the same. I say ye shall be true unto thyself and I shall be unto myself true and unto my trust true. So be it. I am trustworthy. For this am I sent unto thee that the Father's will may be done in me and by me and through me.

I say I am not of a mind to lose my inheritance. So be it I shall finish my mission and return unto my Father wherein I shall abide. And I shall go into darkness no more.

I say I shall never again lower my light, for my work shall be finished in the realm of man. For I say I am finished. I am done. Never again shall I go into darkness. I am now come that it may be complete. So let it. Amen and Selah.

I am come that they may be gathered together and brot out. So be it the Father's will. So be it and Selah. I am Sananda, Son of God.

Recorded by Sister Thedra.

At the Altar -- Father Mother God, what would you say this day to my brother, Metorius?

Sori Sori -- Beloved son: I have sent thee out as my breath made flesh. I say I have sent thee out as my breath made flesh. I sent thee forth as man -- and as man ye became -- flesh. I say ye "became flesh." And as flesh have ye walked blindly. I say ye have gone into darkness and ye have been blinded by the darkness; for once ye were within the realms of light. And therein ye knew all things.

I say it is thy inheritance -- and once again ye shall be as one which knows all things. And I shall be glad. I say I shall be glad. So be it and Selah. Ye shall now walk which way thy crown tilts not and ye shall be as one prepared to go forth in my name and heal them. I say ye shall <u>wait</u> for thy authority, for it shall be given thee and for this shall ye wait.

Now I say unto thee ye shall go unto the mountain - the holy mountain wherein the white altar of alabaster stands, and ye shall remain for a time and ye shall be as one blest, for I have set up my altar there and ye shall go in and I shall speak unto thee and ye shall be blest. So be it and Selah. I am thy older brother, Sananda.

Sori -- Blest be this day. Remember it my children for ye have been truly blest. Will ye not be as ones prepared for thy next part? I say ye shall be blest this night and ye shall come unto the altar on the morrow and I shall speak with thee. Be ye still and at peace. I am with thee. So be it and Selah.

I am Sananda.

Recorded by Sister Thedra.

Sori Sori - Beloved of my being: I bless thee with my presence. I speak unto thee this day for the purpose of giving unto thee the authority and the power to go out among them and to speak that which I would speak -- to speak in my name.

I say I give unto thee the authority to speak for me -- in my name and none shall deny thee. For I shall put within thy hand the rod which shall be made brass. I shall speak and ye shall hear me. I shall give unto thee the word which has been sealed up.

It shall now come forth and it shall be as power; and it shall be for the good of all mankind. So let it be. I am now come that it may be accomplished. For this have I come. I say I have come that this may be accomplished. So let it be.

Ye shall give unto them this word and it shall go forth to bear witness of that which I have said unto thee. And they shall be wise to accept thee in my name. So be it all which receive thee shall receive me and they which receive me shall receive of the Father. So be it and Selah.

I say they which deny my word deny me. They which deny me deny the Father. I am one with him and I am not to be denied. Neither are my hands denied. I say I have called thee forth. I have sibored thee well. I have placed within thy hand the word.

And I have given thee the authority and the power to bless them as I would bless them. I am he which is sent that they may be blest. I am Sananda, Son of God, known as Jesus the Christ - the Son of God am I, born of Mary, ward of Joseph. I am known by the name of Sananda within the temple of light.

So be it ye shall come to know that which has been hidden from thee. I am the Son of God sent forth that there may be light in the earth. So be it and Selah. I am Son of God. So be it and Selah. Adomni Sheloheim.

Recorded by Sister Thedra

Beloved of my being: I say unto thee this day I am within the earth as man made flesh and bone. I come that the Father's will may be done in the earth -- and it shall be. For it is now come when I shall bring together the ones which are prepared to receive me. And I shall train them as soldiers. I shall give unto them the power and the authority to go out before me and to prepare the way before me; and then I shall come.

And I shall bring such light as they have not seen, and I shall give unto them the Crown and the Cross as the symbol of my work. And they shall be blest to be my mouth and my voice. And I shall give unto them the power and authority to set up my church and they shall be counseled by me and they shall have no false gods.

They shall bow down unto no man, and great shall be their reward. I say I shall lay hands upon them and they shall be blest. So be it I am sent that they may be blest. I am come that they may do my work -- that the Father's will may be done in the earth -- that he may be glorified in the earth.

Now I say unto them which are enroute: Be ye mindful of me and I shall go with thee and I shall bless thee. And ye shall listen for my voice and I shall speak unto thee.

Be ye blest of me and I shall come unto thee and counsel thee. I am Sananda, Son of God.

Recorded by Sister Thedra

Beloved of my being: I speak unto thee as a brother, and I speak unto thee as one which has gone before thee. I say I know the pitfalls; I know the heights. I say that as I come unto thee ye shall come unto me; and I say ye shall be free even as I am free. I say ye shall be free even as I am free. I go and come freely, and I know no bounds.

I am forever free and ye shall be as one blest of me and by me, for I say unto thee I shall walk and talk with thee, and I shall speak unto thee in thy own language. And ye shall comprehend that which I say unto thee. I am not a child and I am the one which has been sent that ye may become of age. I say ye shall become of age and ye shall be as one mature for ye shall know as I know.

And ye shall be as one come alive and ye shall be as I am for I am of the Father blest, and I say ye shall walk upright as the Son of God and ye shall be as the one illumined of God the Father and ye shall glorify him in the earth and ye shall be glad forever more.

I say ye shall rejoice forever more. I am now prepared to reveal unto thee many new things which ye have not known (which ye have not remembered). I say ye have forgotten thy inheritance and ye shall come to know that which ye have forgotten. I say ye shall now begin thy new part and ye shall be as one prepared for it.

Ye shall be as my hand made manifest unto them. Ye shall walk among them as I walk. Ye shall lay hands on them and ye shall heal them and ye shall bless them as I would and ye shall do all manner of good works in my name. And for this shall ye be prepared. I say for this shall ye be prepared.

I give unto thee my word I shall come in and counsel thee and I shall give unto thee the power and the authority to speak for me and ye shall lay thy hand on them and they shall be healed. I say, by my grace, shall ye do this. I am now prepared to give unto thee the gift of healing and for this have ye waited. I say ye have waited long for this day.

When ye went into the east from the temple wherein stands the great white altar ye gave a vow ye should return, and ye have wandered afar. Now it is come when ye shall come into the temple of light wherein the one hundred and forty-four sit in council this day for the purpose of bringing this Plan into fullness.

I say it shall be accomplished this day and no man shall stay my hand and no man shall be unto me a stumbling block, for I know what I am about, I know from whence I come and to where I go.

I say I am not deceived by their goodly speech or by their profanity. I know them for that which they are and I say many which say Lord, Lord are not with me. And many which are as the idiots and fools shall be with me in the last day -- for I shall bring them together and I shall touch them and they shall be blest; they shall be made whole and they shall be made to remember all things. I say they shall know as I know.

Now I speak unto thee of the work at hand. Ye shall be as one which has my hand upon thee and ye shall go into thy new place and ye shall begin the part which shall be given unto thee. Ye shall establish a place of refuge wherein there shall come many which are in distress. Many shall come to help thee and ye shall be as one on whose shoulders rests great responsibility -- and ye shall be as one which knows that which ye are to do and ye shall be as one assisted by thy sibors, for we have watched thee and we have assisted thee and we shall continue -- for this is now the time for action.

I say action! And action there shall be -- and now ye shall be as one which can come unto the altar each morning with these words: "Father Mother God, I come that thy will be done in me: by me: through me: and for me." I say unto thee ye shall be as a little child and ye shall follow in my footsteps and ye shall not err, for I shall not mislead thee. I am with thee. I shall direct thee in all thy ways. I am Sananda.

Ye, my beloved, were as my brother wherein ye are at the present time. I say within the holy mountain of Shasta ye were a priest wherein I was the Grand Master. I say I was the Grand Master within the lodge of the brotherhood which is now in session within the holy mountain. I say one hundred and forty-four councilmen now sit within that temple wherein great plans are being made for this day.

And I say ye are part of this plan -- for this are ye now within the place wherein ye are. I say ye shall be gathered together and ye shall be given thy part -- one step at a time -- and as ye fulfill thy part, as ye finish that step, another shall be taken. Such is wisdom; such is growth, and thus thy growth shall be finished and ye shall become an adult and then ye shall begin thy greater part. So be it and Selah. Sananda.

Recorded by Sister Thedra

Beloved of my being: Be ye blest of my being. I come that ye may be blest. Bless each other -- love ye one another as I love thee. Give unto each other that the other be comforted and strengthened. Give unto each other that the light grows brighter. Add unto that light and it shall not die. Be ye blest as the light grows, and ye shall be as priest and priestess within the temple of the most-high living God.

I say ye are priests and priestesses within the temple of the most-high living God. I am the "Priest" and I know myself to be. I speak as such. I walk as such and I defile not my temple. I am the Temple. I go as the one within the Temple. I say: <u>I am the temple</u>. I say: <u>Ye are the temple</u> -- and ye are me. I am thee and we are one -- not three -- not separated -- for we are not the flesh.

We are spirit, and spirit is not divided against itself. I am spirit yet I have come into flesh. I have taken up the flesh as man that ye might know me as man. And I say ye <u>shall</u> know me as man. I say my flesh binds me not. I am free.

And I say unto thee the day of thy deliverance draws nigh when ye, too, shall have thy freedom. And ye shall be as I am. And ye shall know no bondage -- no fear. All shall be thy handmaidens. In love shall the atoms serve thee, for there are none other. Ye are the master. I say ye are the master.

I am the master -- the atoms obey my command. I walk knowingly from whence I came - where I goeth - and what I come to do. I say I know my part and I shall accomplish that which I come to do. Now ye too shall walk the self same path. It is straight and no pitfalls. I say all the law is given within these scripts -- all which is and ever shall be -- for I know the law and I have caused it to be recorded within these scripts for thee. I am not so foolish as to be here for naught. I come that this might be finished -- done -- and that ye may be brought out of bondage.

I gave unto thee a covenant that "I should go and prepare a place for thee" -- and return, that where I go, there ye might go also. Have I not done this? Have I not gone and prepared that place? Have I not returned? Have ye prepared thyself to return with me?

It is now come when many are here upon earth which come even as I am come that ye may return with me. This is the day for which ye have waited. I say it is now come ye shall walk by my side and ye shall counsel with me and ye shall talk with me and ye shall be blest of me and by me. And ye shall know me -- for this have ye waited. I say this is the time long prophesied.

I say ye have come into flesh at this time for this fulfillment of the scriptures. I say it is not accidental that ye are here. I am here also and I know thee. I know where to find thee at all times.

I say I shall call thee by name and ye shall answer me and make haste unto me and I shall quicken thee and ye shall know that moment that which has been sealed. And I say the seal shall be broken and I shall open it up and ye shall not be deceived for we have watched thee and we have assisted thee and we shall continue.

For this is now the time for action. I say action! And action there shall be -- and now ye shall be as one which can come unto the altar each morning with these words: Father Mother God, I come that thy will be done in me: by me: through me: and for me.

I say unto thee, ye shall be as a little child. And ye shall follow in my footsteps. And ye shall not error for I shall not mislead thee. I am with thee. I shall direct thee in all thy ways. I am Sananda.

Ye my beloved were as my brother wherein ye are at the present time. I say within the holy mountain of Shasta ye were a priest wherein I was the Grand Master. I say I was the Grand Masters within the lodge of the brotherhood which is now in session within the holy mountain. I say one hundred and forty four councilmen now sit within that temple wherein great plans are being made for this day; and I say ye are part of this plan.

For this are ye now within the place wherein ye are. I say ye shall be gathered together and ye shall be given thy part one step at a time. And as ye fulfill the part, as ye finish that step, another shall be taken. Such is wisdom. Such is growth, and thus thy growth shall be finished. And ye shall become an adult and then ye shall begin thy greater part. So be it and Selah.

Sananda.

Recorded by Sister Thedra of the Emerald Cross

The above is an excerpt from a communication for one which came to this altar asking for certain information: and is given here with permission:

Beloved ones which I have brought together: I say unto thee I speak unto thee as thy brother -- as one with thee -- and I speak that ye might have these my words. I say ye shall be blest of me and by me. For this have I come. I say I am come that ye may be blest.

Now ye shall remember that which I am about to say unto thee. And for this have ye waited. It is now time to cast aside all thy small ways, all thy childish ways, and come with me. I say ye shall come with me and I shall lead thee into ways ye know not of.

For ye have wandered long and ye have wearied of toil and faint when ye have gone out for long. Ye have passed this way many times and ye have not remembered that which ye have said and done. I say ye have wandered long in darkness. Ye have stumbled and fell. And ye have been unto thyself traitor and ye have been both priest and thief.

Ye have done many things which ye remember unknowingly. I say unknowingly ye remember -- for no experience is ever forgotten -- no vibration lost. And ye have been as ones which have had thy memory blanked from thee, and now ye shall have it restored unto thee and ye shall forgive thyself all thy shortcomings.

And ye shall deny nothing. Ye shall be as ones responsible for all thy misused energy and ye shall transmute it, and do that which has tormented thee no more -- learn from experience and repeat them not.

For I say ye have bound thyself by thy own doing and ye shall now be the one to unbind thyself. And as ye prepare thyself I shall come unto thee and I shall assist thee. For I shall touch thee and I shall bless thee as I have been blest. And ye shall be glad forever more. I am with thee that ye may be blest. I am Sananda.

Recorded by Sister Thedra

Sananda speaking:

Beloved ones; beloved of God art thou. I say unto thee ye are blest to be within flesh this day for I am come that ye may be blest. Ye shall now give unto them this word. And ye shall be blest as I have been blest. So be it and Selah.

Ye shall say unto them as I would, that when the hour strikes I shall step forth with a legion of light workers and I shall declare for the earth her freedom.

And she shall swiftly pass from her present berth into her new port. I say she too shall be freed from bondage and she shall be blest as I have been blest. I say unto them the earth too is ensouled in Spirit -- God the Father -- and she too shall come into her inheritance, and blest shall she be. So be it and Selah.

Now ye shall say as I would that I shall come forth as one glorified of God the Father and I shall glorify all which come into the place wherein I am and they shall be caught up with me. So be it and Selah. I am come that this may be, so be it and Selah. I am Sananda.

Recorded by Sister Thedra

Beloved I speak unto thee this day as one with thee. I speak unto thee that they may have these my words and ye have prepared thyself to receive me. Now I shall speak as one come - for I am come: And I say unto them: I am come for the purpose of giving unto them as I have received. I say they shall be as ones blest as I have been blest. So be it and Selah.

Now give unto them these words as ye receive them. Change no word and bless them with thy part. I say ye shall bless them by thy hand and ye shall be as one blest of me. For I am not unmindful of my servants. I say I am not unmindful of my servants. Give unto them as ye receive and ye shall be blest.

I am now prepared to speak freely, and all which prepare themself shall be blest of me and by me. I am thy Mother Sarah and ye have received me as such, and as such do I speak unto thee. And ye shall be as one brought out of bondage and ye shall know me as I know thee, so be it thy inheritance. And I say ye shall receive in full.

Now ye shall do the work which ye went forth to do -- and ye shall be as one prepared to return home unto me unscathed -- unharmed -- and ye shall be as one made whole, as one purified.

And ye shall know no sorrow -- no pain -- no longing. And ye shall be forever blest. So be it and Selah. I say unto thee my child I have held thee fast in the hours of thy unknowing and in the days of thy wanderings and thy longing.

I have kept thee for this day. And now it is come. I shall give unto thee that for which ye have waited. I say ye have waited long for this day -- and I, too, have waited for thy return unto me.

So be it is now come and I am glad. For it is a glad day when one returns unto their abiding place. Such is the will of the Father that they all return unto me. So be it I am thy Mother God from which ye went out in the beginning.

I am that I am. I am the Father Mother God from which ye came to be. I am thyself made flesh. I am eternal without beginning: without end. I am thy Mother Eternal. I am Sarah.

Recorded by Sister Thedra

Behold me; I come that all things may be made new; I say that ALL things may be made new, so be it and SELAH.

I am with thee this day - and now ye shall be as one brought out of bondage, so be it and SELAH.

I speak unto thee from out the TEMPLE OF THE MOST HIGH LIVING GOD so be it I am thy OLDER BROTHER and thy Sibor Sorica.

SORI SORI: Beloved; It is my part to give unto thee the fore gone and I say unto thee I am not alack; I am not an outcast: I am ONE with the FATHER MOTHER GOD, and I know myself to be; and it is given unto me to be Sorica,--and I am now come unto thee for the purpose of preparing thee for the part which shall profit ALL MANKIND, so be it and SELAH.

I am thy Brother; thy Sister, ONE in SPIRIT; ONE with the ETERNAL PARENT; and now ye shall rise as on wings of LIGHT; and ye shall be blest as I have been blest; ye shall KNOW as I know; and ye shall give unto others as ye receive. I say; as ye receive so shall ye give; and ye shall be blest for thy giving- as ye are blest by thy receiving--such is the law; I say it is more blessed to GIVE than to receive; so be it and SELAH.

I speak unto thee this day of great change: and I say unto thee "CHANGE IS GOOD" and let it be so.

I am now prepared to speak unto them which have a mind to hear:

I say: there shall be great changes and there shall be a lake of FIRE rise from out the mountain within the place wherein there are mighty fortresses; and wherein there are great rivers; and the lake of fire shall be as not seen before. I say: that this shall be before this day is finished; and it shall be when the day is begun; and NOT the end-- I say it shall be BEFORE the end-- and it shall be for a time after the beginning.

Yet I say unto thee, the ones which now hear me, that: THIS IS NONE OF THY CONCERN! For NOT ONE which now reads these words shall be discomforted by this change!

Yet there is constantly changes going on within the terra and ye are not aware of it; for does the babe not grow continually; and does it not become a man? And shall the earth not become ADULT and fulfill her mission?

I say she- the earth- shall come into her own- and she shall throw off the laggards and the sleepers. And she shall be washed in the water of LIFE; and she shall be cleansed; as a wound--and she shall be healed as a wound; and she shall be healed of ALL her wounds, and brought out of her present port into a new berth wherein she shall rest and be as the house wherein the SONS of God may abide.

I say wherein they MAY abide: yet I Say they shall prepare themself for to share in her GLORY, for they shall have free choice wherein they shall serve: they shall go out even as Sananda, and his Brothers have- that thy own wounds may be healed: or they may choose to serve as the right hand of the Father in some distant galaxy- as a star- or a point of LIGHT within the firmaments: and they may even be as one called to serve within the schools of Light wherein the new ones are brought for such initiations as are now taking place within thy own terra, of which the ones yet in darkness know nothing.

I say- of which they KNOW NOTHING. I am aware of them- yet they are not aware of me: I say; I know them; yet they know me NOT- I am not blind- THEY ARE.

I say; they are bound in darkness and they are held fast by their own leg irons which they have forged for themself. They are opinionated; they are bound by the opinions of others and they look not to the SOURCE of their BEING; I say-- they look not to the source of their being for freedom and deliverance.

I say they are burdened down by their own opinions which they have carried with them--which has now become a great shell - enclosing them; they are slow - sluggish; they have not the wings of the free man: THE SWALLOW FLIES, the TURTLE CRAWLS; and so do the sluggish laggards which have the mind of the mass: I say he has not allowed the light to penetrate into his own tower; his own realm; he has drawn a curtain about him; and he chooses his own darkness---

He fears the light- that his way might be changed--he fears change; for the reason he is a laggard: he is OPINIONATED-- and he has the childish mind; he is NOT MATURE-- He is as one bound by foot, and he has not the strength to stand upon the feet of his own.

I say- he shall gain strength to stand alone: I say he is bound by his own THINKING he KNOWS NOT: he THINKS he KNOWS-- and I say-- THERE ARE NONE SO FOOLISH AS THE ONE WHICH thinks HIMSELF wise! I say: NONE so FOOLISH!

I am the one which shall bring unto thee the GREATER PART when ye are so minded to receive it. I am thy Older Brother, Sorica.

Recorded by Sister Thedra

Beloved children: these are the times which have been foretold for many centuries and for which ye have waited; none are brought into this place without reason.

We are all children of the LIVING GOD, and beloved of HIM. Ye have many paths to travel, and have traveled many ways to reach this day; stony paths they have been for the most part; for that seems to be the way which teaches best the lessons ye are here to learn. Walk thy path in PEACE and JOY hard though they be; for the time which is near will find thee prepared to do that for which ye have taken birth. Service to all LIFE is asked of all who are willing to offer themself to that work.

Ye have heard;- THE HARVEST IS HEAVY- AND THE WORKERS FEW -- So it is: and none can be spared who will obey- and follow the Sibors, as they lead and direct.

Not <u>blind</u> obedience; but obedience in the light of understanding: ye will be given the light of understanding and WISDOM; all will be added unto thee as ye have need of. These are the days of sorting; where the tares are separated from the wheat-- the black from the white.

The critical times ahead are for thee to think of -- and to choose WHOM ye will serve. No man cometh unless he desires to come. Ye must ask- it is the law. I am Sananda, Son of God, known as Jesus of Nazareth.

Recorded by Sorea Sorea

The Nazerine Speaks to Montoya and Morona

I Thedra, have before me a letter from Montoya and Norona, from which I quote one sentence: "HOW DO YOU RAISE AN ANGEL?"

As I placed my fingers to the keys of this machine I was aware of the Masters presence; my fingers flew over the keys so swiftly I neither saw nor fully comprehended that which was being written; yet fully aware of his presence.

Beloved Ones:-

How does one raise an Angel? He will help you. Dear ones, this is not a play school--nor is it a kindergarten; though there is a kindergarten for the kindergarteners: you are 'dumped' into the UNIVERSITY with a hood over your eyes- head- and now it is time to be un-hooded and that you see where you are going; and know what you are to do - Yet ye shall hold steadfast to righteousness; and ye shall not lose sight of what you are here for.

Now I have given a command to the beloved one (Thedra) that she is to go to a distant point wherein there shall be many things revealed unto her which shall be revealed unto thee in due time. I say that these are the times which ye have waited for--and now there are great meetings taking place all over the lands and on the seas- that these times may be for the betterment of mankind.

I say that these times may bring forth a new kind of fruit wherein they may eat of the manna which ye have spoken of; and I say MANNA there shall be-- for the ones which are prepared to partake thereof. Now I say unto thee; be ye as the ROCK upon which I shall build my temple; for I have prepared thee for a work, and ye shall be blest of me- and by me: for I come that ye be blest--I say ye SHALL BE BLEST: for have I not sent one unto thee, that he may be given physical form--that he may walk among them as man--and have I not known thee from the beginning?

I say ye shall be as FOSTER parents of the one sent unto thee- and he shall bless thee by his presence- and he shall Sibor thee in Spirit while his vehicle is developing; and then he shall take it and make use of it for the good of all mankind; and yet it shall not bind him for he is a free born man---

Born of God is he: and he shall be no less for taking upon him a vehicle of man-of flesh--for it shall serve him--he shall not be subservient unto it--for I say he shall not be bound by anything--no pore shall hold his spirit- it shall remain eternally free---

Yet is come when they shall have proof that it is come- the age when ANGEL and MAN SHALL WALK SIDE BY SIDE: AND THEY SHALL COUNSEL TOGETHER AND THEY SHALL BE AS BROTHERS: that is the ones which have a mind to be counseled--and to learn- as the ones which I shall send unto him which is to be born this one which ye are to foster--the one known as Moroni--and which shall be called "MARAN"--and which shall take embodiment through one which I have called Morona--and through these of Montoya.

I bless them this day; it is now come when I shall speak unto them as the VOICE- which shall be heard- and it shall NOT be the VOICE in the WILDENESS- but it shall be heard and heeded.

And I say there is a place prepared to bring up this child- wherein shall have the environment which is befitting a Son of God, and he shall be as one trained in the way of the wise--and he shall be called GOOD- and he shall be GOOD--and he shall not be given the BITTER CUP! I say - HE SHALL NOT BE GIVEN THE BITTER CUP!

So be it I have spoken and my hand has recorded this as spoken; and I shall use this means of my work for the present time- and I shall need nothing other than the hands which have dedicated themself to my use: for I am a willing servant of the Father, and as I speak for HIM my servants speak for me---

So be it I shall make of them my "ROYAL ASSEMBLY" and they shall sit with me in the chambers of the council and they shall have the front piece removed, and they shall know as I know: and they shall have no false notions- nor pre-conceived ideas of things Spiritual--of things of SPIRIT--for they shall comprehend them, and they shall be glad this day is come.

I bless thee with my presence- and I anoint thee which is to- and shall be the foster Parents of the beloved Son of God- Moroni, to be called Maran, I am the Nazerine; the Wayshower, I have spoken- yet I am not finished I shall speak again. SELAH.

Recorded by Sister Thedra

IN OBEDIENCE

SORI SORI: BELOVED OF MY BEING: -

I AM COME THAT YE MAY BE BLEST SO BE IT AND SELAH

I SAY UNTO THEE- I AM NOW PREPARED TO BRING THEE INTO THE PLACE WHEREIN I AM: AND I SAY YE SHALL SEE ME FACE TO FACE

AND YE SHALL BEAR WITNESS OF ME--AND YE SHALL RETURN—THAT YE MAY BE UNTO THEM THE MESSENGER- FOR HAVE I NOT MADE THEE MY MESSENGER?

I SAY YE HAVE DONE WELL, SO BE IT AND SELAH. I SAY YE SHALL BE AS ONE WHICH SHALL RETURN UNTO THEM AND YE SHALL SAY UNTO THEM: "IT IS COME WHEN THE LORD THY BROTHER SANANDA, WALKS THE EARTH-- FOR I HAVE COUNSELED WITH HIM AND I HAVE SAT WITH HIM AND I KNOW WHERE OF I SPEAK, SO BE IT AND SELAH."

I SAY YE SHALL GIVE THIS TO THEM-- AND YE SHALL GIVE IT AT THE EARLIEST POSSIBLE TIME, SO BE IT AND SELAH. I AM SANANDA.

SISTER THEDRA.

Beloved ones: which I have brought together: I speak unto thee of a plan- and a place. I am now prepared to speak unto thee of many things: and I say as ye are prepared so shall ye receive. Now be ye prepared: for I am about to speak unto thee of a place wherein ye have not been; and ye shall go into that place- and therein ye shall find many which shall be therein- and ye shall know them for I shall cause thee to remember them- and ye shall be glad for thy memory.

Now ye shall be as one prepared- for within the days just ahead ye shall depart from the place wherein ye are- and ye shall journey into the North Country and therein ye shall find a place which is prepared for thee - and therein ye shall learn of me; and I shall give unto thee a plan whereby ye may return unto them- and ye shall give unto them as ye have received.

I say- ye shall return unto them- and ye shall give unto them as ye have received, so be it and SELAH. Now ye shall give unto them this word and ye shall be as one wise indeed to be as my mouth and as my hand; and I say I shall lead thee from the place wherein ye are unto the place wherein I am.

And I say I am with many of my Brothers from the realms of light which have come even as I am come-- and I say we are not of a mind to betray our self or our trust--for it is willed of and by the Father Mother God that this be accomplished; that this plan be brought into its fullness.

And I say many are called- and few are chosen; and the ones which are chosen-- are so chosen for their part because they have proven themself trustworthy-- and they have gone the long way to bless them which are yet within the realms of darkness.

So be it I am prepared to give unto thee the gift of healing- and I say ye shall heal them of their infirmities - and of their blindness - and ye shall lift them up, and ye shall be unto them all that I shall be unto thee so be it and SELAH.

I shall give unto thee thy reward- and I say again; MY SERVANTS DO NOT GO UNREWARDED: I AM NOT OF A MIND TO FORGET THEM. I AM HERE: I AM HERE! And I shall bring thee into the place of my abode- and I shall bring thee as one of earth; and I say- ye shall find thy way as such, yet ye shall return unto them the wise one, so be it and Selah.

I am thy Brother and thy Sibor, Sananda.

Recorded by Sister Thedra

Beloved: I bring unto thee one from out the South which I have prepared for this part - and I say unto thee; he is my hand and my mouth and he shall be thy hand and thy foot; for I send him unto thee that he may be such. I say ye shall be as his sister - and he as thy brother, and ye shall go into the North country as one prepared - and ye shall be as one which has earned thy passport.

I say - ye shall be as one prepared for this place - and all things shall be in order. I say: All things shall be in order --- I am within the place wherein ye shall go - and I say, ye shall be as one prepared to return unto them - ye shall be as my messenger; and ye shall bring unto them the message that I am here; I AM COME; and ye shall say unto them: "HE IS COME - I HAVE BEEN WITH HIM, AND I HAVE COUNSELED WITH HIM".

Now I say ye shall be unto them my messenger--and ye shall bear witness of Me, and ye shall go out from the place wherein I am as one befitting my messenger - for I shall touch thee - and I shall prepare thee for that which shall be given unto thee to do, so be it and SELAH.

I am thy Sibor and I have sibored thee well - so be it and Selah. I am now prepared to receive thee into this place which is the School of Melchizedek, and which is the place wherein ye shall remain for a short period - and that is not as ye count days ---

It is not as ye count weeks yet is for the duration of the work which is to be done. Ye shall return unto them as my messenger: I say it shall be within and ye shall be as one prepared within that time; I say ye shall be as one prepared in that time and ye shall return unto them, so be it and SELAH.

Ye shall bring them together at the Altar and ye shall counsel with Me and I shall speak unto thee - and I shall say that which I have waited to say--so be it and SELAH - I am at thy service - I am Sananda. (Thedra)

Behold Me

I come that ye may be prepared for this part; and I say ye shall be prepared, and now ye shall be blest as ye have not been blest; ye shall go into the place wherein I am and ye shall stand before me as one prepared; and ye shall be as one on whose head rests a crown - and ye shall return unto them and bring unto them that which I shall give unto thee for them-- and they shall not deny Me - for I say, I SHALL PROVE MYSELF: and they which demand proof shall be as the FOOLISH ones yet I say I shall prove myself.

I go that ye may follow Me - I am with thee - and I am glad - I am as thy Brother Sananda.

Recorded by Sister Thedra

Behold Me: I come unto thee this day for the reason - the Father has sent me; and for the purpose of bringing thee out of bondage. I say ye have prepared thyself for thy new part; and ye shall now be brought into the place wherein I am--and ye shall be as one blest of me and by me - for ye shall learn of me - and ye shall be as one prepared for the Greater Part; and ye shall return unto them and give unto them as ye have received, so be it and SELAH.

I am now prepared to bring thee into the place of my abode wherein I shall train thee according to thy part; and wherein ye shall find many which have come even as I, that ye may be prepared. I say ye shall let thy present activities cease for the time - and ye shall pick up again when ye return unto them - and they shall be as ones blest to receive thee; I say; "they shall be as ones blest to receive thee" - so be it and SELAH.

I say when ye return unto them ye shall bless them as I would; and ye shall be as my hands and my feet: and ye shall say unto them - "HE IS COME" and ye shall give unto them as they are prepared to receive so be it and SELAH. I am thy Brother and thy Sibor, Sananda - Sori Sori.

Recorded by Sister Thedra

With All Thy Learning Get Understanding

BEHOLD ME I COME- that ye may be given this part- and I say ye shall give it unto them as thy own: now say unto them as I would; that ye shall depart from them for a time- and it shall be for the good of all mankind--and ye shall be with me- for have I not said SO? I say it is SO! So be it I have given unto thee much for them--now they have it-- and they shall alert themself, and be aware of that which goes on about them--and they shall be responsible for themself.

I say they shall be as ones responsible for themself: they shall apply that which has been given unto them through thee. I say; ye shall now come into the place of my abode and I shall sibor thee in thy next part--and then- ye shall return unto them and give unto them as they are prepared to receive.

I say: "AS THEY ARE PREPARED TO RECEIVE" so be it and SELAH.

I have said this is no time for the laggards; they shall wait their time. It is the Will of the Father they ALL come from out the darkness yet they will it not! And so be it that we thy Sibors wait their preparation; and when they are sufficiently prepared we shall reveal our self unto them so be it and SELAH.

I speak for thee:- and I say; ye shall come into my place of abode as ye are- and ye shall return unto them as one made new- and ye shall be as such: I say ye shall walk among them KNOWINGLY.

I AM with thee- and I shall not fail thee--be ye blest this day--I am not afar off. I am thy servant and thy Sibor Sananda the Nazerine.

SORI SORI; BEHOLD ME-I AM HERE! I AM COME: I AM COME.

I speak unto thee this day as one in flesh and bone: I AM HERE! I walk the earth as man--and I am thy Brother which has gone before thee to prepare the way for thee- that where I go ye may go also.

I now say unto thee my beloved Thedra, that it is now come when ye shall come into my place of abode and ye shall be instructed of me- and by me ye shall be given the laws which they know not: I say they know <u>me</u> not! Neither do they seek me out! They are not of a mind to follow me: they seek signs and wonders! They are opinionated: they run to and fro seeking of them which know NOT. They are as blind- and deaf.

I say, they ask of them which know me NOT! I say: PITY ARE THEY- I AM HERE! yet they believe <u>ME</u> <u>NOT</u>! I SAY--I AM--I AM- -and they are as ones looking unto the day when GREAT SIGNS shall appear in the heavens! ARE THEY NOT? Are they aware of that which goes on about them? I say -- ye shall be as one prepared for the next part--and ye shall give unto them as <u>they</u> are prepared to receive: grieve not for the laggards: grieve not for the traitors: be a lamp unto their feet- and walk which way <u>thy</u> <u>crown</u> <u>tilts</u> <u>not</u>!

And follow in my footsteps, and ye shall be VICTORIOUS- for this do I say- ye are my hand and my foot: for I know thee; I am not deceived by appearances, I bless thee this day, I am with thee, I say be ye blest by all which do sit in council with me. I am thy Brother and thy Sibor Sananda.

Recorded by Sister Thedra

SORI SORI - BEHOLD ME: I AM THYSELF WHICH IS ETERNAL WITHOUT END-- FOREVER SHALL I BE - I AM THE MIGHTY ONE--I AM THE KEEPER AT THY GATE, THY GATE I STAND; AND I GUARD WITH DILIGENCE--AND I SAY UNTO THEE I AM - AND I DO NOT FAIL - NEITHER DO I SLEEP: ARISE! AND COME UNTO ME AND SLEEP NO MORE.

I SAY COME UNTO ME AND SLEEP NO MORE - I BID THEE COME: LEAVE THY LEG IRONS AND SOAR INTO THE PLACE WHEREIN I AM; LET NOTHING BIND THEE: GIVE THYSELF THAT YE MAY BE BLEST OF ME SORI SORI. BEHOLD ME THIS DAY - WALK YE IN SILENCE KNOWING I AM WITH THEE--- PRAISE YE THE NAME OF SOLEN AUM SOLEN.

BEHOLD ALL THINGS MADE NEW

BE YE AS ONE BLEST - I SHALL DO MY PART - WALK WITH ME THIS DAY GUARD WELL THY DOOR FOR ONE SHALL COME WHICH WOULD TRY TO DESTROY THY PEACE-- BE AWARE OF ME AND I SHALL STAY THEE--

I AM HE WHICH NEVER FAILS--

I AM THE ALPHA AND THE OMEGA-- HAIL IT IS SO---SO BE IT AND SELAH.

I SPEAK AS MAN -- I WALK AS MAN--

I SHALL COME UNTO THEE AS MAN AND

I SHALL NOT FAIL MY MISSION

I SHALL BE TRUE UNTO MYSELF AND MY TRUST FOR I KNOW MYSELF TO BE-- I AM ONE WITH MY FATHER MOTHER GOD SOLEN AUM SOLEN- SOLEN BE PRAISED - LET IT BE SO - LET IT BE SO!

PRAISE BE THIS DAY - REMEMBER THIS DAY AND KEEP IT HOLY - I AM.

BELOVED: I HEAR THEE: I KNOW THEE AND THY CAPACITY: I AM NOW PREPARED TO BRING THEE INTO THY NEW PLACE WHEREIN YE SHALL WORK IN PEACE AND WITH DIGNITY - SO LET IT BE.

I SAY IT IS THE FATHER'S WILL THAT YE BE PUT INTO ANOTHER PLACE WHEREIN YE SHALL ABIDE IN PEACE AND HARMONY --I SEE THAT WHICH GOES ON BEHIND LOCKED DOORS -- I KNOW THAT WHICH THEY SAY AND DO - AND I AM ALERT FOR I GO INTO THE RECESSES OF THEIR HEART AND I SEE THAT WHICH IS THERE - AND I SAY THEY HIDE NAUGHT FROM ME - NAUGHT!

NOW I SAY YE SHALL PREPARE THYSELF FOR THY NEW PLACE WHEREIN I SHALL BRING UNTO THEE MY SERVANTS AND MANY SHALL FIND THEIR WAY UNTO THY DOOR.

NOW YE SHALL BE ALERT FOR I SAY YE SHALL BE AS ONE FACED WITH ONE WHICH HAS THE WILL TO DISTURB THY PEACE--NOW YE SHALL BE POISED--FOR THE TIME IS COME WHEN YE SHALL BE GIVEN THE BITTER CUP--SO BE YE AS ONE WHICH HAS MY HAND UPON THEE--I SAY YE ARE NOT ALONE, SO BE IT AND SELAH. BLEST SHALL YE BE,

I AM, SANANDA.

Recorded by Sister Thedra of the Emerald Cross

Moroni speaking:

Behold Him the Son of God known as Sananda --

BEHOLD HIM! HE IS COME! I say HE IS COME: I know him--and I am come too-- come as one yet in embryo: I say I am -- even before I was flesh--yet I AM <u>no less</u> for taking upon myself the vehicle of flesh substance. I AM - eternally the same--ONE with the Father Mother God.

I speak unto thee my beloved this day as the ETERNAL that I AM--I speak as SPIRIT of Father Mother God I Am.

I AM within the place wherein all things are known.

I say ye shall stand as one unveiled; as one which has gone this way for the last time. I say ye shall be delivered from the wheel of rebirth--I am not bound unto it; yet I am in embryo--I shall make my entrance within the world of men at the appointed time---

And I shall grow to maturity as it is accustomed to them--I shall be unlike them--inasmuch as I shall have my memory -- and I SHALL BE FREE--I shall not be bound--I shall go and come freely. I shall be a freeborn man--I shall be unto myself sufficient---

I shall teach my foster parents--for I shall be unto them watcher: I shall come unto them for that purpose--I shall be unto them the

WATCHER; I shall bring unto them great wisdom and knowledge--I shall bless them--for this do I come--I say I am come to bless--and to give unto the world that for which they have waited---

I am with thee that ye may be blest--and I say ye shall go into the distant land and ye shall therein learn many things for which ye have waited. I say thy reward shall be great.

I am now come that ye may know that which I can give unto thee: for this have ye prepared thyself--I say as ye prepare thyself so shall ye receive. I bless thee with my presence--and I say ye may send this my word abroad the lands-- for the word shall bear witness of me--and I say none shall deny me for I say they shall be as the foolish ones; for I am now prepared to come as flesh and bone--and I shall prove myself.

And I say it is not given unto me to withhold this part from them-- I give it freely--and the ones which have a mind to comprehend shall be glad it is come when I shall bring into their midst a body of flesh that my word may become perfected within the earth--I have waited for this day--so let it be as a cause for great joy--for I bring light from the realms of light---

I am of the Father Mother God sent that He may be glorified in this age-- I say in THIS AGE! And too I say it shall be accomplished through US -- HIS SONS -- HIS DAUGHTERS---

Moroni.

BE YE RESPONSIVE UNTO HIS WILL -- Praise ye HIS name -- the name of Solen Aum Solen is <u>POWER</u> -- <u>ALL</u> <u>POWER</u>. Use it -- for the good of all mankind -- bless thyself with it -- bless them with it. Be true unto thyself -- ask naught of man -- for HE is ever at thy command-- and bless HIS NAME-- Command of them obedience unto the law -- which is LOVE - PEACE - and HARMONY. Be unto them a lamp and cast not thy pearls before the unjust and the UNGODLY for they are the anti-CHRISTS.

Be ye as one which can comprehend that which I say unto thee-- Peace and Poise unto thee my beloved - hold steadfast unto righteousness and I shall bless thee with my presence -- PEACE -- PEACE --

Sori Sori - Sons of God are we. AUM SOLEN. I AM MORONI.

Recorded by Sister Thedra

Beloved of my being -- give unto me the one thing I ask of thee -- thy Love -- thy recognition of my presence. For it is now come when ye shall come to know me; as ye shall know many of my brothers and sisters of light. I am one which has watched in silence--I am known as MARCHUS-- on the hill whereupon I abide I am known as the watcher of the little ones.

I keep watch -- when the day wearies them; their toil ended--I draw near unto them -- I give unto them comfort wherein they may find rest-- I bless them with my presence--and I am not afar off--for there is no separation in LOVE -- I AM LOVE IN ACTION -- I speak unto thee of LOVE for this have ye waited; I say ye have waited long for this.

I am now prepared to come unto thee as one made manifest, and I shall speak with thee and ye shall be glad--I am with thee in spirit -- yet

I shall come in flesh -- and for this have ye waited. I am thy brother Marchus.

Recorded by Sister Thedra

Speaks to his parents: thru the Spirit--

Beloved Ones: Whom are ONE today:- I speak to thee a greeting of Love and goodwill. Has it not been said that I would come? and am I not here in the vehicle of flesh and bone? I am he--I am Mayran--I am come into the world of darkness -- yet there shall be no darkness around me--I am come to sibor them which have a mind to listen, and comprehend what I am sent to do.

Be ye patient Oh wards of my vehicle--be ye at PEACE--and I will guide thee step by step--I am come to bring thee out of darkness; yet I say ye shall free thyself--ye shall be as ones made whole, for ye shall know and be aware of the FATHER'S WILL at all times.

I say ye shall inherit HIS will and glad ye shall be, so be it and SELAH I am come to guide thee so be it and Beleis. I am come as one of flesh and bone yet I am not bound by flesh; I am free as the WILL is free - ye shall be the same - decree it - and it will be so, so be it and Beleis and Selah.

I am come in the LIGHT of the Christ, which ye shall realize and know. I am come for the benefit of all who have eyes to see - ears to hear - and wisdom to comprehend; and I say wise indeed are they who will listen - hear and comprehend the FATHER'S WILL - I am come to bring peace and LIGHT and LIFE eternal.

I AM Mayran.

I AM HE

Behold me thy GOD: which has sent thee out: and I say unto thee I have given unto thee BEING- I bless thee this day--

I speak unto thee as man that ye may comprehend that which I say unto thee--

I AM thy Father Mother

I AM not divided--for I AM thy Father, Mother, Brother, Sister, thy Child and thy Servant.

I AM the Greatest and I AM the Smallest--

I AM thyself- thou art me - BEHOLD ME! and ye shall KNOW ME!

Be ye rational in thy knowing- for from me ye are not - and ye know thyself to be -- be blest in thy knowing--

Let me be thy shield and thy buckler--

Walk with me - talk with me- and dwell forever with me--

For I say unto thee there is no mystery except thy un-KNOWING-

SO be ye as one prepared to receive me - and of me-

For I say unto thee:

I AM all things - both great and small-

I AM that which is - was - and ever shall be!

Behold me thy GOD; thy armor in battle; thy bread in the hours of hunger- thy solace in the time of sorrow--thy love--thy freedom--thy ALL

I AM; BEHOLD ME! And I shall make of thee GOD OF THY WORLD - I SHALL GIVE UNTO THEE MY SHIELD - AND I SHALL CROWN THEE WITH MY LIGHT – I SHALL PLACE UPON THY HEAD MY HAND - AND I SHALL GIVE UNTO THEE THE AUTHORITY AND THE POWER TO BLESS THEM AS I WOULD HAVE THEE BLESS THEM.

BEHOLD ME! I reveal many things unto thee and ye shall remember all things which I reveal - let it be thy inheritance. I AM not afar off - I AM nearer than thy hand and thy foot for I AM that which ye shall come to know - the eternal I AM PRESENCE which thou art - ALWAYS - ETERNALLY - without END!

LO I AM with thee this day - go where I go - let it be thy light which leadeth them out of bondage - for I have no other light than thee---

For thou art me - I AM THEE--

Wander no more apart from me -- behold me thy GOD for beside ME there is NAUGHT!

I am thy Father SOLEN AUM SOLEN:

Recorded by Sister Thedra of the Emerald Cross

SORI SORI: BEHOLD ME THY GOD, I AM: AND I AM COME THAT THERE MAY BE LIGHT IN THE WORLD OF MEN.

BEHOLD MY HANDIWORK AND I SAY UNTO THEE IT IS MIGHTY - IT IS GREAT: IT IS GIVEN UNTO ME TO KNOW THY CAPACITY AND I SAY YE SHALL BE AS THE ROCK UPON WHICH I SHALL BUILD MY TEMPLE. I SHALL BUILD IT FOUR SQUARE AND I SHALL BUILD IT UNTO THE ETERNAL I AM PRESENCE - FOR I AM THE PRESENCE - I AM THE ALL FROM EVERLASTING UNTO EVERLASTING - I AM NOT CONSUMED BY TIME - NEITHER AM I DIMINISHED BY TIME - I AM - I SHALL REMAIN EVER THAT WHICH I WAS -

I AM THOU - THOU ART ME - I AM NOW PREPARED TO EXPRESS MYSELF

THRU THEE, AS MY SELF - I AM - NOW YE SHALL GO INTO A NEW PLACE

OF ABODE WHEREIN YE SHALL DO THE WILL OF THE FATHER - YE SHALL BE

AS MY HAND AND AS MY MOUTH AND YE SHALL BLESS THEM AS I BLESS

THEE - SO BE IT AND SELAH - NEVER FEAR - AND YE SHALL BE AS ONE

BLEST OF ME AND BY ME - I AM WITH THEE BY DAY AND BY NIGHT AND I

SAY YE SHALL NOT FAIL NEITHER SHALL YE FALTER -

THE LION SHALL ROAR AND THE WINDS SHALL HOWL-

THE FOREST SHALL BEND UNTO THE HOWLING

YET YE SHALL BE UNMOVED -

I AM THY FATHER SOLEN AUM SOLEN

LET THY LIFE BE MY LIFE

AND I SHALL FREE THEE WITH GREAT JOY -

FOREVER AND FOREVER.

BELOVED OF MY BEING: BE YE BLEST THIS DAY AND YE SHALL BLESS

THEM AS YE HAVE BEEN BLEST: NOW YE SHALL GIVE UNTO THEM THIS WORD AND THEY SHALL RECEIVE IT IN MY NAME, AND THEY SHALL GO FORTH AS MY HAND AND MY FOOT - AND THEY SHALL WALK AS I WALK, THEY SHALL SPEAK THAT WHICH I GIVE UNTO THEM TO SPEAK AND THEY SHALL DO MY WORK AND SHALL BE UNTO THEM GREAT LIGHT.

I SAY YE SHALL GO INTO THE PLACE WHEREIN THERE SHALL BE SOME GATHERED TOGETHER FOR THE SAKE OF LEARNING, AND THEREIN YE SHALL FIND THEM AND I SHALL PUT MY WORDS INTO THY MOUTH AND I SHALL NOT FAIL THEE - NEITHER SHALL YE FAIL---

I SAY GREAT IS THY WORK AND YE SHALL BE AS ONE ON WHOSE SHOULDERS RESTS THE RESPONSIBILITY OF MY

WORK: I SHALL NOT HOLD THEE RESPONSIBLE FOR THAT WHICH THEY DO WITH MY WORDS--YET YE SHALL BE AS ONE RESPONSIBLE UNTO THYSELF FOR THIS PART; BETRAY NOT THYSELF.

I SAY GO YE INTO THE PLACE WHEREIN THEY GATHER AND SPEAK MY WORDS AND I SHALL REWARD THEE IN LIKE FASHION.

BLEST ART THOU THIS DAY - BLEST SHALL YE BE-- AMEN, AMEN, I AM;

THOU ART I AM - I AM THOU--WE ARE ONE.

BLEST SHALL YE BE--AUM SOLEN-AUM SOLEN - PRAISE THE NAME OF

SOLEN AUM SOLEN.

Recorded by Sister Thedra of the Emerald Cross

Bor speaking: Let thine light so shine that all may see--

Let thine heart rejoice this day

Let thine eyes behold his glory

Let thine eyes see the work of his hand

Let thine ears hear that which he doth proclaim

Let thy feet be swift to do his bidding

Let thy hands bless all things which they touch

Let thy mouth proclaim his truth

Let thine arm be strong in his work

Let thy word be HIS word for

Has he not given unto thee the power of speech that

Ye might glorify him in the earth?

Be ye as his hand his foot his voice--

And ye shall know him as he is--

So be it and it is so. I know;

I am he who has been with him thy Father God

Which has sent thee out. So be it and Selah.

Blest shall ye be this day. Go ye from the place wherein ye are into thy new place wherein ye shall go as ones prepared. For I say ye shall have a new dwelling place. So be it and Selah. Blest are they which walk blindly and falter not. I am Bor.

Recorded by Sister Thedra of the Emerald Cross

SORI SORI - I SPEAK UNTO THEE AS ONE OF OLD-I SPEAK UNTO THEE OUT THE FULLNESS OF TIME - I SPEAK UNTO THEE AS FATHER TO CHILD - I SPEAK UNTO THEE AS

MOTHER TO CHILD--I AM THY MOTHER, AND I AM THYSELF: THOU ART ME, THERE IS NO DIVISION, NO SEPARATION - ONLY THY THINKING MAKES IT SO: YET IT IS NOT SO! FOR IT IS BUT AN ILLUSION, IT IS THE GREAT ILLUSION CREATED BY THE WHORE---

FOR I SAY UNTO THEE YE SHALL COME TO KNOW ME THY FATHER MOTHER GOD, CAUSE OF THY BEING - LET NO MAN TELL THEE YE SHALL <u>NEVER</u> KNOW ME: FOR IT IS <u>NOT TRUE</u>! IT IS THINE INHERITANCE TO KNOW ME, FOR HAVE I NOT SENT THEE OUT? YET YE HAVE FORGOTTEN: YET THY FORGETTING MAKES ME NONE THE LESS - FOR I AM THY FATHER MOTHER, I HAVE CRADLED THEE WITHIN MY HEART, I HAVE HELD THEE FAST WITHIN THE HOURS OF THY FORGETTING - IN THE HOURS OF THY WANDERING - IN THE HOURS OF THY LONGING.

NOW I SAY YE SHALL RETURN UNTO ME UNSCATHED UNHARMED FOR I HAVE KEPT THEE FOR THIS DAY. NOW I SAY YE SHALL GO FOR TH AND DECLARE MY WORDS - YE SHALL DO MY WORK AMONG MEN ---

YE SHALL DO MY WILL, FOR I HAVE SENT THEE FORTH FOR THAT PURPOSE: AND I SHALL GLORIFY MYSELF THROUGH THEE.

I SHALL BLESS THEM THROUGH THEE -- I SHALL LIFT THEM UP AND I SHALL BRING THEM INTO THE PLACE WHEREIN I AM, WHEREIN THEY SHALL KNOW ALL THINGS.

I SAY UNTO THEE IT IS THY INHERITANCE <u>WILLED</u> UNTO THEE FROM THE BEGINNING SO BE IT YE SHALL ACCEPT IT AS THY INHERITANCE, I AM THY FATHER: AM I NOT A JUST FATHER? DO I NOT PROVIDE FOR MY CHILDREN?

BE YE NOT DECEIVED - I SAY I AM A JUST FATHER; BE YE BLEST OF ME AND BY ME. HEAR ME O, MY CHILDREN, BE YE NOT DECEIVED BY THE WHORE WHICH IS THE ILLUSION, LET IT PASS FROM THEE.

MIGHTY ARE MY WORKS, MIGHTY - MIGHTY! BEHOLD MY HAND MOVETH UPON THE LAND, AND MY BREATH SHEDDETH ITS PART ABROAD IN THE LAND ---

MY HAND REACHETH INTO ALL THE LANDS OF THE EARTH, AND I PEOPLE ALL THE LANDS. -- I SEND THEM FORTH THAT THE LANDS BE PEOPLED: AND I PREPARE THE LANDS, AND I PROVIDE FOR THEM - YET THEY SAY THERE IS NO GOD!

I SAY THEY ARE FOOLISH CHILDREN, BOWED WITH THE BLACK CAPE: THEY ARE WITHIN THE FOG OF ILLUSION.

I SAY: LIFT UP THINE EYES MY CHILDREN.

I SAY ARISE COME UNTO ME AND I SHALL RECEIVE THEE UNTO MYSELF.

I AM A MERCIFUL FATHER, HEAR ME! HEAR ME! I COMMAND OF THEE HEAR ME! RETURN UNTO ME THIS DAY!

I AM THY PARENT ETERNAL.

SOLEN AUM SOLEN.

Recorded by Thedra of the Emerald Cross

Beloved Children of Mine:

I speak unto thee this day as thy Mother Eternal - I bless thee as such-- Now ye shall be unto each other much comfort - and ye shall walk together as my children, while I feed thee from my breast---

I shall bless thee with my life - I shall sustain thee in all thy time-- I shall sustain thee thru all thy trials - and all the storms of earth for I AM thy <u>Mother</u> <u>Eternal</u>---

I AM she which has carried thee within the womb of time --

I AM she which has given unto thee being--

I AM the one which has nourished thee ere ye came into thy present body, or vehicle of flesh--

I AM she which has held thee fast in the hours of thy UNKNOWING - in the hours of thy sleep---

I AM she which now quickens life into thee --

I AM now ready to receive thee into my place of abode wherein

I AM - wherein ye may receive thy second birth--I say: Ye shall receive thy second birth--and ye shall not taste of death for

I AM now prepared to give unto thee the water of life--

I say: One shall walk among thee prepared to give unto thee of the crystal goblet--

I say: Within the goblet ye shall find the water of life--and when

ye see one holding within their hand the crystal goblet

ye shall ask of that one to drink-- say unto him <u>MAY</u> <u>I</u> <u>DRINK</u>:

and when ye have drunken of the liquid light ye shall step forth

from thy old body of earthly substance as one made new, as one made whole and NEVER again shall ye be bound by the bonds of earth.

Ye shall be as a free born man-- so let it be.

I say it is so; for I KNOW all things which are hidden from thee-- yet that which is hidden shall be revealed unto thee -- so be it and SELAH.

Now ye shall remember me and that which I have said unto thee and ye shall remember that which I have reminded thee of--ye shall give thanks unto thy benefactors for thy welfare -- all that which has given unto thee comfort; and ye shall give unto thy SOURCE credit for being THY BEING--and ye shall give unto thyself credit for being my SONS--my DAUGHTERS --my CHILDREN which I love-- I guard - I trust - Be ye trustworthy - betray not thyself or thy trust-- Be as wise as the serpent -- let my life flow thru thee and I shall glorify myself in thee and thru thee -- let it be <u>my</u> <u>life</u> which shall glorify thee---

I have spoken this day--and I shall speak again and again-- Let it be for the good of all my children - who know me not - I say they are bound in darkness--yet I am ready and SO WILLING to deliver them out.

I AM thy MOTHER ETERNAL. SARAH AM I,

Recorded by Sister Thedra

Beloved of my being: I now speak unto thee on such as is my part. I say it is given unto me to see them in the place wherein they abide with the wanton and the willful ones which do sway their minds. Now I say ye shall be as the rock and ye shall be as the foundation upon which I shall build my temple. I say ye shall be as the foundation upon which I shall build my temple. For I say ye shall stand as the rock.

Now let it be recorded that I have set my seal upon thee and I have appointed thee the priestess whom I shall give unto thy keeping such knowledge as shall be unto them their shield and their buckler, their shibboleth and their succor. I say they which do endure shall be forever blest.

So be it that thy days shall be short within thy present place of abode and ye shall be put into another place wherein ye shall do my work. Now ye shall be as one which has my hand upon thee and ye shall be blest of me and by me.

Now I speak unto the one which I have sent to shield and to guard thee. I say unto him I am mindful of him and I shall reward him in like me a sure. Now I say unto my beloved who has served me, she shall be glad for this day and she too shall be rewarded in like measure.

I say blest are they who follow in my footsteps blindly; blest are they which walk with me while knowing not. I say I AM COME. I AM WITH THEE; yet ye see me not. Lo behold my handiwork. I am He which has directed thy journey and I know that which has been done. So shall ye come to know it is so, and I say so.

I am Sananda.

Behold me this day. My plans are not always clear unto thee nor are my words. Yet I clarify them as time dictates. I say I clarify them as time dictates for this do ye become aware of my way and of thy oneness with me. I say ye are one with me and ye shall say that which I give unto thee to say and ye shall be blest.

Now first I speak unto thee of Spirit which is the first fruit. Second I speak unto thee of Action -- and action there shall be. Spirit moves thee into action and that action shall bear the fruit thereof. Submit thy will unto the Father's and nothing shall prevail against thee. For His Will *is* the great plan for it is the perfect plan.

Go ye not unto the foolish Virgins for oil -- they have none; they have brought forth no sons; no fruit have they brought forth. Now ye shall bring forth sons which shall raise them up and they shall be unto me my hand my foot and great shall be my joy. Lift up thine eyes -- behold mine hand move upon all the land.

I cast aside the veil of darkness; I rend asunder thy bonds which have held thee fast. Behold me! For I speak unto thee from the fullness of my being. I say thou art me for I am thee and ye have given of thyself that I might come in and sibor thee. I say I shall take up my abode herein and nothing shall dispossess me. I am the hand of my Father which has sent me.

My Father and I are one yet he is greater than I. And I am thy Father in him yet he is greater than we. Yet ye and I are equal in him and for this day shall ye be glad when ye too shall be delivered out even as I. I am free even as ye shall be free. Lo it is so for I have decreed it so. And so be it.

Before thee stands a mighty host which shall protect thee when thy trials are unbearable; when thy days are fraught with care. Yet ye shall be unto thyself true and ye shall be victorious and ye shall glorify the Father in the earth. For this have ye come. Lot it is so. I am here; I am with thee. Be ye at peace and poise. I am Sananda.

Beloved ones which I have called forth. I now say unto thee, arise and come forth! For have I not said that I am within the earth as flesh and bone? Have I not spoken unto thee as man? Have I not given unto thee of the substance of things hoped for?

Have I not given unto thee signs? And have I not done that which none other has done? Have I not said that "greater than these shall ye do?" Now hear me in this -- Am I not a sensible man? Would I mislead thee? For have I not kept my covenant with thee? And have I not returned unto thee that ye may be brought out of bondage?

I say I am not a traitor; neither am I a liar. Be ye rational in thy reasoning. And I ask of thee, would I be so foolish as to forfeit my inheritance? For I have received my inheritance in full. So be it I shall be unto my trust true and I shall give unto thee as ye are prepared to receive.

Now ye shall stand firm unto them nothing which they can use against thee and give no ground, for I say ye have won thy laurels the hard way. Be ye as one prepared to go forth to slay the dragon and wear well thy cloak of authority: for ye shall not flaunt thy learning before man.

Wear well thy badge of authority and wise ye shall be. Be ye as wise as the serpent and silent as the Sphinx. Lo, ye shall see me and accept me for that which I am. I am he who has waited for this day. I am Sananda Son of God.

Recorded by Sister Thedra of the Emerald Cross

Sori Sori - Behold me this day, and see that which I acclaim unto thee.

See that which I do--

See that which ye shall do--

See that which has been done --

See that which they do--

And be ye not alarmed for their unknowing--

Know ye the power of the word

And use it for the good of all mankind--

Let not thy substance be wasted and let not thy knowing be troubled--

For I have planted my feet upon the earth that they may be sustained that they may be better for the knowledge which I bring. I say that the knowledge which I bring shall become common knowledge unto all mankind which so wills it.

Now drag no more thy leg irons. Arise ye and walk in freedom; be ye bound no more in darkness.

I say be ye bound no more in darkness for I come that ye may have light.

Let thy light be my light

Let thy time be my time

Let thy life be my life

Let thy cross be my cross

Let my sacrifices be thine

Let my joy be thy joy

Let my freedom be thy freedom.

Arise from thy own part which has been unto thee thy cross; and come with me. Help me carry my cross and wait no more; for I do declare for thee thy freedom forever and forever.

And ye shall now rejoice that this day is come; for I say great shall be thy joy.

Give unto me credit for knowing that which I say unto thee. I am with thee that ye may come unto the place wherein I am as my very own. I say ye have been true unto thy calling and I shall deliver thee out. So be it and selah. I am Sananda.

Maroni

Beloved of my being, I am Maroni:

And this day ye have walked with me. Hold fast unto me and I shall bring into focus that which shall become thy greater work. Ye shall now wait for the greater part for a time - when the work has gained momentum and when the foundation is finished and when they are stronger. I say their backs shall be strengthened. And they shall carry the load; then ye shall go out from them and ye shall leave it in their care. So be it and Selah.

I am now prepared to give unto thee a part for them and it shall prepare them for the greater part. And ye shall be as my hand and as my mouth unto them. Be ye as such for it shall be thy good fortune. I am the one which is this day come as babe - which has taken form of babe - yet, I animate that form: babe is not the Spirit. Spirit animates the form. And I am not bound by form.

Will ye not comprehend this? And I say, I use many. So be ye not deceived. I am form, I am spirit; yet I animate form. Spirit changes not, is none the less by the forms which it uses. So be it and Selah. I am now within the earth as babe; and as such I shall grow into maturity; and as such as man I shall go out and administer unto them, and I shall finish that which I began so long ago. My work is not finished for it is a large task, a long mission which I have chosen.

I say that there will be some changes made and change is good. For Spirit knows no stagnation and there is no stagnation in me, for I am Spirit. I am Action. I am the Spirit sent forth that this plan may bring fruit. I say, that this babe I have brot forth is my vehicle that this day may come into its fullness; that it may bring forth fruit which shall glorify the father upon the earth.

I say that the edifices which they set up of their own accord and name them for the saints and for themselves is not the Spirit: not the Holy Ghost. Neither is it the body of God the Father. I say: "Ye are the church": "Ye are the temple of the Living God." Ye are the Spirit - the "I Am" - the presence of the Living God is the Spirit which is the "temple." The house is but the instrument which is but a footstool for the Sons of God.

I say, ye are the "temple" -- keep it clean -- purify it -- use it for the glory of Him which has caused us to be. Praise His Holy name -- the name of "Solen Aum Solen" is pure unadulterated. Keep it holy. Speak it. Praise the name and it shall bring unto thee peace. Be ye wise in thy judgment; perceive that which is done. Let not thy knowing trip thee up. Let thy knowing be wisdom from the wisdom of the Almighty God which has endowed us with all his fortune. Be ye of good cheer. We know thy needs and we are with thee. Lo it is so. So be it and Selah.

I am thy sibor Maroni

Recorded by Sister Thedra

Sori Sori: The day is come - the time is now--

Ye shall sing forth thy praise unto the Father of hosts!

Arise oh mighty Ones!

Gather thy flocks from the fields

And be glad this day is come---

Arise oh Mighty Ones!

Sing ye the songs of praise unto the Lord of Hosts--

Almighty he is which keeps watch this day--

Hear me - Oh Mighty Ones -- Fear not that ye are forgotten--

Praise ye the name of Solen Aum Solen--

Mighty is his name --

Give thanks this day is come--

Call from the rooftops - from the mountain tops

That they may hear thy voice

HE IS COME! HE IS COME!

Arise ye hosts - join the hosts of the earth

Sing ye the glad tidings

Rest not on thy laurels

We shall begin the New Day with a gladness of heart

And a swiftness of speech--

And a knowing which surpasses all wisdom of ages past.

Arise! and rejoice He is now come the Lord of Hosts.

Praise ye the name of Solen Aum Solen.

Recorded by Sister Thedra

Sori Sori: Behold me: I come as on the wings of the dawn. I speak with the voice of the angelic host. I am the Lord of hosts. I speak unto thee and ye hear me. I am nigh unto thee. I keep thee in the hours of thy unknowing. I am he which stands porter at thy gate. I await thy bidding. I say I move upon thy command. I say, command of me that which ye will and I shall comply. Behold the power of the word and let it be for the good of all mankind. I say let it be for the good of all mankind. Allow it to be.

Ye shall now forget that which is done. And it shall be forever cleansed from thy record and remembered no more. Forgive thyself all thy wanton - all thy shortcomings - and Arise - as on wings - and claim thy inheritance. So be forceful in thy knowing. Know that thou art the Sons of God the Father. Walk in his light. Wear thy shield which is Light. Wear his shield which is thy protection. Seal thyself that no thing of darkness shall touch thee.

Give ye thanks for this day and be glad. I am come that ye may walk in the way I set before thee. Be ye blest of me and by me and ye shall go where I go. So shall it be.

I am thy sibor and thy elder brother, Sananda.

Pour out thy love upon them which do spitefully use thee. Blame them not, for they are the unknowing ones. Whisper unto them in the hours of their sleep. Say unto them that they shall be brought into the light of the father-mother when they so will. Be ye as one which holds them close in thy light. Sweeten thy own cup with thy own knowing. Bless them as I bless thee. I deny them nothing yet they do turn from me. They have given unto thee the bitter cup yet it shall be sweetened by thine own knowing and glad shall ye be.

Behold my hand moveth swiftly and ye shall see the perfection of the plan -- lo it is so; give thanks in all things.

Be ye blest this day. I am with thee. I am Sananda.

Recorded by Sister Thedra

Sori Sori - Light of the world am I. "I Am" - let nothing dim thy sight of me.

Be ye as the light which I am

Let thy light shine as mine

Be ye as one glad and be ye as one prepared to receive me.

For this do I now speak unto thee that ye may be prepared.

Now I say unto thee I come as man yet I am that which "I Am"

My form hinders me not, neither am I bound by form.

Do I resist forms -- NO -- I am independent of form -

Yet I use form for that which I choose to do.

Be ye as one which can see beyond appearances.

I am the Life and I am the resurrection.

Let thine thoughts be staid upon the Presence which is the "I Am" the "Life" -- and ye shall be as one qualified for thy next part.

Let thy life be devoted unto the new life. Let each day be a new day.

Drag not thine leg irons -- Free thyself from all bondage, all dogmas, all creeds. Let thine light break forth from the mist. Praise ye the name of Solen Aum Solen. Give thanks thy freedom is given thee. Lo it is so. I am Sananda.

SORI SORI - Behold the majesty of my hand -- it is great -- for therein is power -- therein is light. Be aware of the power -- Be mindful of me -- for I abide with thee---

I AM the knower - and the doer--

I AM he which awaits thy bidding--

I AM he which serves thee by day and by night--

I AM he which has spoken unto thee in the hours of thy sleep--

I AM he which stands guard at thy gate that no unclean thing enter therein

I AM the light

I AM the way - and it is now come when mighty shall be thy work, for it shall bring forth fruit of a new kind - and ye shall know the wisdom of thy waiting--

Let not thy spirit linger for I say ye shall ARISE as on wings of the dawn

Behold my handiwork for I say it is good - so be it and Selah

LO, I have seen thee as ones frail and as ones untrained of my ways.

Yet I say ye shall come to know me and my work - my way - for this do I now bring unto thee this word--

Ye shall go into a place wherein ye shall find one which has prepared for thee a part and he shall instruct thee in that part and ye shall go forth as one prepared - and for this ye shall be blest--

Now ye shall give thought unto that which I say unto thee--I am now prepared to come unto thee and instruct thee in thy new part-- be prepared--and I shall speak unto thee at length on this subject. I am Sananda.

Recorded by Sister Thedra.

Maran speaketh- with my life I bless thee for I am come as one called Maroni - I have taken upon myself the body of flesh- and of flesh, as flesh- that the Word might become understood by Man - for Man comprehends little of Spirit- and of Spirit I shall speak while it is yet early- it is later than they Know I Say that they Know Not that which goes on about them and they are as babes at the breast-

I Say that I am now, Come that I Might Walk Among them as Man- as Man I Shall Walk - yet while the physical vehicle grows unto Manhood I shall lead the way and prepare them for my Ministery. This Shall be done in Spirit from the realms of Spirit, and I Say that the Spirit which is ever the Same - is not bound by that which is flesh- and yet they See the flesh and call it Man- So let it be according to their understanding- Yet I say I shall give unto them New and greater understanding for I am sent of the Father that this may be- and when Ye go into the land of the Mormons wherein they have erected the great tabernacle. Ye shall find one which has a mind to hear and he shall be one which shall give unto thee a hand and ye shall be as one which shall be led unto him and he unto thee- I am now prepared for this day- Yet I am the babe- and I am Not of earth be Ye of a Mind to comprehend- that which I say unto thee I am Maroni

Maran

Recorded by: Thedra

Sori Sori: The day is come - the time is now --

Ye shall sing forth thy praise unto the father of hosts!

Arise oh Mighty Ones!

Gather thy flocks from the fields

And be glad this day is come---

Arise oh Mighty Ones!

Sing ye the songs of praise unto the Lord of Hosts--

Almighty he is which keeps watch this day--

Hear me - Oh Mighty Ones --

Fear not that ye are forgotten--

Praise ye the name of Solen Aum Solen--

Mighty is his name --

Give thanks this day is come--

Call from the rooftops - from the mountain tops

That they may hear thy voice

HE IS COME! HE IS COME!

Arise ye hosts - join the hosts of the earth

Sing ye the glad tidings

Rest not on thy laurels

We shall begin the New Day with a gladness of heart

And a swiftness of speech--

And a knowing which surpasses all wisdom of ages past.

Arise! and rejoice He is now come the Lord of Hosts.

Praise ye the name of Solen Aum Solen.

Recorded by Sister Thedra

Sori Sori: Behold me: I come as on the wings of the dawn. I speak with the voice of the angelic host. I am the Lord of hosts. I speak unto thee and ye hear me. I am nigh unto thee. I keep thee in the hours of thy unknowing. I am he which stands porter at thy gate. I await thy bidding. I say I move upon thy command. I say, command of me that which ye will and I shall comply. Behold the power of the word and let it be for the good of all mankind. I say let it be for the good of all mankind. Allow it to be. Ye shall now forget that which is done. And it shall be forever cleansed from thy record and remembered no more. Forgive thyself all thy wanton - all thy shortcomings - and Arise - as on wings - and claim thy inheritance. So be forceful in thy knowing. Know that thou art the Sons of God the Father. Walk in his light. Wear thy shield which is Light. Wear his shield which is thy protection. Seal thyself that no thing of darkness shall touch thee.

Give ye thanks for this day and be glad. I am come that ye may walk in the way I set before thee. Be ye blest of me and by me and ye shall go where I go. So shall it be.

I am thy sibor and thy elder brother, Sananda.

Pour out thy love upon them which do spitefully use thee. Blame them not, for they are the unknowing ones. Whisper unto them in the hours of their sleep. Say unto them that they shall be brought into the light of the father-mother when they so will. Be ye as one which holds them close in thy light. Sweeten thy own cup with thy own knowing. Bless them as I bless thee. I deny them nothing yet they do turn from me. They have given unto thee the bitter cup yet it shall be sweetened by thine own knowing and glad shall ye be.

Behold my hand moveth swiftly and ye shall see the perfection of the plan -- lo it is so; give thanks in all things.

Be ye blest this day. I am with thee. I am Sananda.

Recorded by Sister Thedra

Sori Sori - Light of the world am I. "I Am" - let nothing dim thy sight of me.

Be ye as the light which I am

Let thy light shine as mine

Be ye as one glad and be ye as one prepared to receive me.

For this do I now speak unto thee that ye may be prepared.

Now I say unto thee I come as man yet I am that which "I Am"

My form hinders me not, neither am I bound by form.

Do I resist forms -- NO -- I am independent of form -

Yet I use form for that which I choose to do.

Be ye as one which can see beyond appearances.

I am the Life and I am the resurrection.

Let thine thoughts be staid upon the Presence which is the "I Am" the "Life" -- and ye shall be as one qualified for thy next part.

Let thy life be devoted unto the new life. Let each day be a new day.

Drag not thine leg irons -- Free thyself from all bondage, all dogmas, all creeds. Let thine light break forth from the mist. Praise ye the name of Solen Aum Solen. Give thanks thy freedom is given thee. Lo it is so. I am Sananda.

SORI SORI - Behold the majesty of my hand -- it is great -- for therein is power -- therein is light. Be aware of the power -- Be mindful of me -- for I abide with thee---

I AM the knower - and the doer--

I AM he which awaits thy bidding--

I AM he which serves thee by day and by night--

I AM he which has spoken unto thee in the hours of thy sleep--

I AM he which stands guard at thy gate that no unclean thing enter therein

I AM the light

I AM the way - and it is now come when mighty shall be thy work, for it shall bring forth fruit of a new kind - and ye shall know the wisdom of thy waiting--

Let not thy spirit linger for I say ye shall ARISE as on wings of the dawn

Behold my handiwork for I say it is good - so be it and Selah

LO, I have seen thee as ones frail and as ones untrained of my ways. Yet I say ye shall come to know me and my work - my way - for this do I now bring unto thee this word--

Ye shall go into a place wherein ye shall find one which has prepared for thee a part and he shall instruct thee in that part and ye shall go forth as one prepared - and for this ye shall be blest--

Now ye shall give thought unto that which I say unto thee--I am now prepared to come unto thee and instruct thee in thy new part-- be prepared--and I shall speak unto thee at length on this subject. I am Sananda.

Recorded by Sister Thedra.

Maran speaketh- with my life I bless thee for I am come as one called Maroni - I have taken upon myself the body of flesh- and of flesh, as flesh- that the Word might be come understood by Man - for Man comprehends little of Spirit- and of Spirit I Shall Speak While it is yet early- it is later than they Know I Say that they Know Not that which goes on about them and they are as babes at the breast-

I Say that I am now come that I might walk among them as man- as man I Shall Walk - yet while the physical vehicle grows unto Manhood I shall lead the way and prepare them for my Ministry. This shall be done in Spirit from the realms of Spirit, and I Say that the Spirit which is ever the Same - is not bound by that which is flesh- and yet they See the flesh and call it Man- So let it be according to their understanding ---

Yet I say I shall give unto them New and greater understanding for I am sent of the Father that this may be- and when Ye go into the land of the Mormons wherein they have erected the great tabernacle Ye shall find one which has a mind to hear and he shall be one which shall give unto thee a hand and ye shall be as one which shall be led unto him and he unto thee- I am now prepared for this day- Yet I am the babe- and I am Not of earth be Ye of a Mind to comprehend- that which I say unto thee I am Maroni

Maran

Recorded by: Thedra

EVENING MEDITATION

My voice I raise in PRAISE! - I sing a glad anthem - for it is now come that man has at last received me! - I am come from out the silence as a holy benediction upon the Earth - and upon mankind - be ye blest of me and by me - for this have I descended into Hell --

I have come that ye may arise and come forth even as Lazarus did come forth from the tomb! I say unto the race of man - ye shall arise and come forth - ere ye are cut off from ETERNAL LIFE and cast into outer darkness forever. Blame not another power for thy slothfulness - for I say unto thee - ye have FREE WILL - use it for thy own salvation --

Hear ME! Oh, ye Children of Earth! Arise! shake off thy lethargy and come home - Abide with ME, in the house of the Lord - for HE shall reign forever - and ever - was it not written thusly? And it is so - or I should not say it!

Beloved - I say unto thee - give unto thyself credit for hearing my words and being as one capable of receiving them perfectly - for this have ye been prepared - I say unto thee mighty shall be thy work and great shall be the fruit thereof.

Great shall be the fruit of thy labors - and too - I say ye have labored long and lovingly - yet thy love shall encompass the nations and all peoples of Earth and yea - the Heavens - for they shall open up unto thee - and great shall be the host thereof - for they shall gather and sing glad hosannas unto the Father - for His mercy and His love throughout all the Cosmos, and ye shall be as one caught up with ME in the Glory of the New Day.

I AM HE which is come - I AM BORN - I AM HE which is come. I AM HE which is made flesh by the spoken word - so be it I AM HE, which shall be the KING of KINGS - Let it be - I AM ---

Recorded by Sister Thedra

I Am He

Beloved of My Being : --

By my hand shall ye be blest this day--I say unto thee- ye shall be blest this day- so be it a great day!

I say, not one has recognized the POWER of the "WORD" and they have not used it for themselves. I say; that when the WORD is spoken as it was intended- it shall bring to them the blessings which they expect from me---

For this has it been given- so be it the law--I give it - thou takest it- what dost thou do with it but bless thyself? Thou hast asked that I bless thee--I give it- yet it lies dormant within thee-- USE IT! and declare for thyself "I AM HE" which has sent me.

I AM the door

I AM the thought

I AM the provider- and the receiver

I am the consumer- and the consumed

I AM HE who goes out

I AM HE which goes not

I AM at rest - and

I AM HE which moveth upon the waters

I AM HE which has nothing-needs nothing and I have all things for

I AM all things--created I them-both great and small

I AM He which has created thee--for

I AM thou- thou art ME- recognize thy own DIVINITY and return unto me!

I gave thee this fiat when ye first went from me- so be it I have not changed it-- thou shall return unto me--- I WILL IT SO--so be it as I WILL IT! return unto me VICTORIOUS! and the VICTORY shall be a GLORIOUS ONE!

So be it I have spoken--and I shall speak again -and AGAIN!

I AM SOLEN AUM SOLEN - thy ETERNAL FATHER.

Recorded by Sister Thedra

Awaken All Ye Nations

Beloved of my being, let nothing stay thy footsteps- make haste and give unto them this word---that it is nigh upon them when they shall see with their natural eyes that which has been done in the hours of their unKNOWING---their foolishness!

I say that it is now come when they, the ones which THINK themself WISE shall be brought to account for their foolishness- and their own willfulness!

I say, they have given unto themself the bitter cup!

For <u>no longer</u> shall we THE COUNCIL of TWELVE - THE COUNCIL of SEVEN sit by and watch which has been set into motion become another scene of Melchizedek! I say that the energy which has built up within the earth- about the earth shall soar up through- around and about the surface of the earth as a mighty eruption---a quake as they have not known!

I say, they have not given unto us- their benefactors credit for knowing that which we say! They heed not our warning! And they heed not the Laws of God the Father!

I say, there are MIGHTY COUNCILS - Councils which have been set up, put into action which deals with such things- where JUSTICE and MERCY is dealt out unto all--

I say that the JUST and RIGHTEOUS shall not suffer at the hands of the unjust and unrighteous! I say - that it is now cone when they shall be caught up short- for they have <u>THOUGHT- themself wise</u>! They have called MY PROPHETS "CRAZY" - they have persecuted them - they have flaunted <u>their wisdom</u> in the face of MY PROPHETS!

I say, it is finished! - for my hand moveth---and I stand in the seat of JUDGMENT! - and I AM a righteous JUDGE---And no MAN shall be unto me a tack in my shoe! For the earth IS MINE! I bow unto no man- for I AM HE which created the earth- and the fullness thereof!

I say - I SHALL NOT ALLOW MINE HANDIWORK TO GO FOR NAUGHT!

I say, this day shall ye get this word into their hands- and I shall speak through many a hand- voice-channel- many an instrument have

I, too. I command each one of them- COOPERATE IN THIS MY WORK---be unto me another finger- for ye are mine hands---

And if one of mine fingers offend me I shall pluck it off- and grow anew! <u>Be ye not so foolish</u> as to <u>think</u> I speak foolishly- for I AM thy GOD which has sent thee forth into flesh- I AM HE which has breathed LIFE into thy animate form---

There is no foolishness in me!

I command thee, each of my fingers "MY CHILDREN OF EARTH" hold fast unto mine Laws---love ye one another---work as one---cooperate in spreading these my Words---and GREAT shall be thy reward!

I say, bless thyself as ye would that I bless thee---

I say, I AM thy Father---I gave unto thee BEING---

Behold my handiwork! Lift up thine eyes! Give unto me credit for my good Work---for I have created thee perfect-- Why art thou so doleful? I bid thee ARISE! RETURN UNTO ME and I shall give unto thee thy inheritance in full---

Praise ye the name of Solen---I AM HE---I AM thy shield and thy buckler--- I AM thyself ---be not so FOOLISH as to misuse the Life-ENERGY---which I have endowed unto thee---for I say unto the, Oh, foolish Ones - that my hand is not shortened!

That which I have given I can take---that which I have created I can destroy---I say unto thee, be NOT SO FOOLISH as to <u>THINK</u> ye know me for to know me is to LOVE ME!

I reveal not my precepts unto the foolish- which <u>THINK</u> themself wise!

I say - I AM a just Father- and I shall not see MY CHILDREN which doeth LOVE me with all their hearts, destroyed by thy willfulness!

HEAR ME! ALL YE NATIONS OF THE EARTH! ARISE FROM THY SLEEP! Shake off the barnacles---cut away thy leg-irons! And return unto me---And I shall accept thee in LOVE AND MERCY---

I AM THY FATHER, MERCIFUL AND LOVING---

Solen Aum Solen.

Messenger---Thedra.

Initiation

Beloved: this day mine hand rests upon thee- and I bless thee with my BEING: for have I not brought thee hence- have I not given unto thee being of my own free will? Now let it profit thee to return unto me -- and I shall crown thee with mine own hand and ye shall wear the Royal raiment- and ye shall be caught up with the host of mine Angels/Mine Sons, which shall be gathered in at the time of the harvest---

I say unto thee; great is this day- for my hand moveth upon the face of the earth- and mine voice have I raised against the wicked and the unjust- and I have commanded them to halt their way of willfulness; and to give unto me credit for their BEING--and I have commanded them to be mindful of all my Mercy/ my Love/ My laws!

And I have spoken unto the just -- and the SMALLEST of these is wise, beyond the greatest of them which do think themself wise! And they which do sit in "high" places and torment My People---

I say unto thee My Daughter, they shall be brought low- and the lowly shall be exalted above them--and 'they' shall be as ones brought low-'they' shall be faced with their own willfulness and foolishness! For I say- "THERE ARE NONE SO FOOLISH AS THE ONE WHICH THINKS HIMSELF WISE." So be it- and Selah.

I say unto him: he shall be as one faced with his foolishness- and he shall be found wanting- for he shall fall short his course! I say: I AM the JUDGE OF RIGHTEOUSNESS! I AM not deceived --for I know them for that which they are --and that which they do--for I have given unto them Being!

And I say they have turned their face from me - and they have not remembered me- for they are in darkness- and their memory has been blanked from them--yet I say they shall be as ones prepared to have it returned--for this shall they wait for my word--for my hand to move for I shall know when they have reached the age of accountability wherein they are responsible for all their actions--all their own deeds-- and when it is come that they are so prepared I shall touch them and they shall be quickened and their memory shall be returned unto them--

I say the record is sealed up- and they have not eyes to see- nor ears to hear--- Yet I am aware or all that goes on in their hearts and many doth serve Me diligently while not remembering Me-- yet I say, that more GLORIOUS is it to serve ME while walking blindly -- for I say he shall be rewarded a thousand times-thousand: for I say greater is his reward which serves me with all his MIGHT--all his Heart - than he which has not gone out from Me ---

The ninety nine- which remaineth with Me shall not know such glory as the <u>ONE</u> which went out- and returned unto Me of his own free will I speak unto thee a parable of truth-- and of he which goes out and returns unto Me-- for to him I shall give the keys of My Kingdom I shall make him the keeper of the records---

I shall give him My Royal Raiment--and I shall clothe him with the Sun--and I shall bring him into the place wherein I AM-and I shall bless him as none of the others- for he shall be the VICTOR -- and I AM his God which has done the work for he has surrendered his will unto me that I might raise him up-- and so be it.

I shall in this day- destroy all their illusions of death- and I shall lift them from their sleep--and I shall give unto them the water of life- and they shall drink thereof- and then they shall step from their bodies of dense substance- into their bodies of Light substance as one forever free- and it shall not bind them- and they shall arise as on wings of LIGHT and be free even as I AM free and they shall return unto Me at will- and they shall abide with Me forever-more!

Was it not said that I am a <u>Merciful</u> God- and who can deny it? I say I Am a patient Father--I LOVE my Children! Yet I do not the things which they do-- for they are the foolish little ones-- who have lost their way-- I say: LOOK UP! OH, YE LITTLE ONES; BEHOLD ME FOR I AM THY FATHER!

Ye remember Me only in thy longing for PEACE and JUSTICE- for ALL MANKIND! I say- put aside thy self--thy strife--thy pride--

thy hypocrisy--thy <u>wonton</u>--(rebelliousness) and return unto Me-- and I shall give unto thee from the fullness of my Mercy and LOVE---

My LOVE knows no bounds --My Patients endureth - yet! 'THY Time' grows short: for I shall close the door again: and ye shall wait another day (AGE) Yea, many days have ye waited ere ye went from Me---

I bid thee thee make haste- ere it is closed-- for it has closed upon their hands before this day---

I say, that I am not or a mind to wait again for "THY TIME" --- This is MY DAY! And I have sent mine Emissaries --mine Sons- that ye may awaken-- Now ye shall heed that which they say unto thee--- I do not send FOOLS to Sibor thee-- for I am not one of thee-- I AM thy Father! All WISE/ALL-POWERFUL-- J<u>U</u>ST- beyond thy comprehension!

And I say ye know me not--for to know Me is to LOVE Me---and to LOVE Me is to keep MY LAWS-- and to keep my laws is to receive thy inheritance in full--and to receive thy inheritance in full is to receive thy GODHOOD---

Be ye blest this day and be ye as One free from all darkness-- let thy mind be MY MIND! and I say- I shall crown thee with mine Glory so be it and SELAH---

I AM THY FATHER ETERNAL---SOLEN AUM SOLEN

At the last hour they shall rush to the gate -to find is close then they shall cry out Lord! Lord! hast thou forgotten me? and I shall answer saying: depart - for ye know me not" From the scrip of the SIBORS.

Mine Son! Mine Son!

Beloved of MY Being: I spake unto thee - and thou hast heard me- I say unto thee, ye shall be my hand made manifest unto one of mine Sons which hast not ears to hear me- and whose eyes have not opened unto mine glory---

I say unto thee; ye shall be mine hand made manifest unto him- and say unto him as I would- could he hear mine voice - I AM in the place wherein he shall be brought- and he shall be as one prepared- for he shall stand before me as one unbound-- he shall be as one freed from all limitations of physical manifestations--of earthly vibrations- and he shall soar as on wings of light- and he shall see and hear as I see and hear---

I say unto him- he has forgotten his days of freedom wherein he did sit in the temple of Light wherein there is no bondage---

I say, he has had his memory blanked from him--and too- I say unto him- it shall be restored! So be it a glad day!

Now let it be said; that it is now come when great and might shall be his work-- for he shall lay aside that which is temporal and base-- he shall be as one prepared for the greater part- and he shall walk as one which has a crown upon his head- and he shall walk which way it tilts not---

I say- he shall prepare himself for that which shall come to pass- and I say- he, this mine Son, which has come unto mine scribe from out the East shall walk as "MAN" among men! He shall walk upright and I shall call him by name "..." and he shall hear it and answer when it is called-- and he shall say unto me: "HERE AM I FATHER! I HEAR THEE--USE ME FATHER AS THOU WILL." Be it so - and so be---

I say unto him; I AM not afar off- I AM nigh unto him- and I say it is not I that sleepeth-- yea- it is my SON that sleepeth! Yet I say my Son shall awaken! And he shall arise! and come unto me as one ALIVE! AWAKE! and he shall no longer wander in the valley of despair-- in the wilderness of time--and the maze of confusion wherein they are tormented---

I say unto him; ARISE! MY SON! AND SEE ME IN ALL MINE GLORY! FOR THE GLORY OF HEAVEN AND EARTH IS MINE!

I say that all things of Earth shall pass away into the elements from whence they came - yet nine glory shall endure forever and forever! Behold mine handiwork- for this have I given thee eyes- which are as yet closed unto such glory--yet I say unto this mine Son- that thine eyes shall behold mine Glory!

I say- My SON! ARISE! And return unto me and I shall crown thee as my own-- and I shall be glad it is done--for long have I awaited thy return -- I say unto thee Mine Son-- thou art the root of Jessie- and the seed of David--and thou art dear unto mine heart- for I have sent thee hence that ye nay fulfill thy mission which ye did begin so long ago? I say unto mine Son I shall see it through-- Be ye not jealous of mine Sons which I have sent to find thee- to awaken thee that ye may return unto me-- but alert thyself - and give thanks that this day is come when ye shall know- and know that ye KNOW!

Holy! Holy! is thy name-- remember it- and defile it not! For I say unto thee- I have spoken, and this mine daughter/ mine hand made manifest hast heard me and responded- and ye shall respond as she- for I say- great shall be thy work and finished thy mission! So be it-- and I say unto thee- it is <u>NOT</u> finished at this hour!

So be it that there is yet time- yet time is running out-- that which ye refer to as "TIME" -- I AM not limited by time- or space- for I AM time--I AM 'SPACE' I AM- 'ALL'--ALL THINGS both manifest and unmanifest-inanimate--and animate-- both seen and unseen-- both large and small

I move in the ether as Light--I AM the waters that cover the deep-- I Am the depth--I AM the height-- I AM the boundless--I AM the boundless- I AM HE which knows all things--yet I AM the sleeper--I AM he which sleepeth-- for from myself have I created him which doth sleep!

Wherein is thine understanding Oh, Mine Son-- that thou hast not known these things-? I say unto thee- AWAKEN! AWAKEN! and return unto me! And I shall endow thee with all that I AM! And ye shall wander in darkness no more-- neither shall we know pain or suffering of any manner.

I say mine arm is long and strong-- and I shall pluck thee from thy bed and I shall spit upon thine eyes and they shall open unto mine glory and ye shall leap up for joy- that at last ye have seen me-- and ye shall not return into darkness again- for I say unto thee Mine SON; it is finished- and ye shall return VICTORIOUS!

Ray of my LIGHT art thou-- and see that it grows ever brighter and that all men may see it and walk by it -- I say unto thee- make straight way that they may follow in thy footsteps, and that they may awaken--

I say ye shall glorify Me in the Earth- that I might glorify thee as a SON returned unto Me--and the GLAD HOSANAS shall ring out "HAIL! A SON IS BORN IN THE EAST! AND HE HAS RECEIVED HIS ETERNAL FREEDOM! HAIL! HE HAS RETURNED AT LAST! "

And there shall be such joy as ye have not known! Let it be so for I have decreed it! Be ye blest Mine Son--I have said it so shall it be!

Solen Aum Solen.

The messenger

Great is My Name - Solen Aum Solen

Albeit I Am He which hast heard thy supplication- and I say unto thee GREAT is the POWER thereof - for am I not alert unto thy supplications which thou hast made unto Me?

I say unto thee: Mine arm is long and strong and I weary not in well doing- nor do I tire of giving of Myself- for there are none which I have sent forth which I have forgotten-- I say unto thee BE YE AS MINDFUL OF ME AS I AM OF THEE AND YE SHALL WALK WITH ME AS MINE-- AS ONE KNOWING---

And I say unto thee - ye shall not be deceived for there is no deceit or deception within Me- I say unto thee great is My name- and great the power thereof - and nothing shall withstand the power thereof which is opposed unto it- Be ye mindful of this and call forth My benediction on them which doth spitefully use thee-- Bless them with MY WORDS - MY NAME- for this have I given it unto thee---

Force not thine own will upon MINE- and forget NOT that I AM the ALL WISE- ALL POWERFUL GOD of the WORLD- GOD of the firmaments GOD of the HEAVENS- for have I not created the Heavens and the Earth-have I not filled them with MY handiwork?

Have I not peopled the Earth with all the races- colors- all the peoples which have turned from Me- and which shall now turn unto Me as ONE people! I say they shall be as ONE PEOPLE- for this have I visited upon them MY handiwork- and for this doeth MY law become manifest -- And I say they shall be bound together by one common bond- that of suffering- and not one which hateth his brother shall escape the law that he learns- and too, I say- that a lesson learned is a lesson earned---

And great shall be their suffering- for this shall they be bound together as by the ties of one common bond- that of LOVE- and they shall come to Me as "ONE"- and they shall be as ONE within ME-- For within ME are NO races- NO colors- NO creeds- NO divisions - I AM NOT DIVIDED- I AM not in PARTS - I AM the WHOLE- the ALL-- I AM from EVERLASTING to EVERLASTING--

And I say unto them which do turn their face from Me- they shall know great sorrow for this is the fortune which they have fortuned upon themself - they have chosen their way- yet they shall ask of Me deliverance and I shall hear them and deliver them out- So be it and Selah-

I AM thy Father

Solen Aum Solen

Recorded by Sister Thedra

He is the Judge

Beloved: I am now prepared to receive thee into the place wherein I am and hast thou not asked of Me - that MY WILL be done? And done it shall be -- For I shall bring thee into the Place of My abode and ye shall be glad - for long have ye waited this day!

Now ye shall receive one into thy house which shall have MY Hand upon him - and he shall be as a brother - and ye shall receive him as such - for I shall say unto thee he is My hand and My foot made manifest for this part which I give unto him - his part is no small part - for I have sent him as My fore-runner that he may make way for Me - and that he might make the way clear that I might come in and abide in their citadels - and that I might speak unto them-

Yet I say they have closed Me out - for they do sit in the seat of judgement and judge unrighteous judgement - I say they judge unrighteous judgement - they pronounce judgement upon MY PEOPLE which I call out and which I do give the Voice of Prophecy.

I say - they which do sit in high places and which have set themself up by their own authority have closed Me out! And they know Me NOT! I say - THEY KNOW ME NOT!

Neither do they prepare themself for to receive Me - I give unto the lowly and the just the "Voice of Prophecy" and the tongues of Angels for they speak MY WORDS - and their mouth is sweetened - for they are not filled with venom- and they revile not MY PROPHETS and they sit not in the seat of judgement for that alone belongs to the Father God - God the Father - Source of Our Being!

Let it be understood - NONE OTHER takes from HIM this seat - this OFFICE - for it is HIS ALONE! NONE can usurp it!

Be ye sure of HIS PLACE! And know them by their fruits --

I say unto thee My Child: I am He which is made flesh by the spoken Word - that I am come - I Am in the Earth made flesh that there might be Light - and I bring with Me a Host of Sons of God which hast received their freedom even as I - And Their part is that of Mine - to bring Light - and so shall it be for and unto all which doth expect Us - Our gifts - the gifts of Our Father God - I say we shall walk amongst them - We shall speak in words which are designed for their understanding - for their own good - welfare --

And I say - that they which have come as My forerunners shall be as ones rewarded - for theirs is indeed a sad task! And I am in no way glad for their suffering - yet - their reward shall be a glorious one indeed.

When the Brother of which I speak comes unto thee ye shall greet him thusly".." and ye shall be blest - Be ye as My mouth and as My hand unto him and give unto him this My word - and Ye shall commune one with the other - and I shall preside as thy Elder Brother So be it and Selah. I Am He which is known as Sananda, Son of God.

- - - - - - -

Note: Let none other believe himself to be this brother - "to come" He is well identified - it is accomplished, Recorded by Thedra

Sananda's Easter Message

Beloved of My Being:-

I AM the Lord - thy Brother - which has been called by many Names - and by many signs have I identified Myself -- And now I speak unto thee for the good of All mankind - that they, the children of the Earth may awaken - and come forth from out the tomb - and that they may arise from a condition of lethargy - and sleep ---

I say unto them - I AM the ARISEN LORD - the Lord of Hosts AM I -- For I Am now Come -- Into the Earth have I descended - even as into the darkened sepulcher have I entered ---

And I say unto them - AWAKEN! AWAKEN ALL YE WHICH DOTH SLEEP! FOR I AM COME! I AM COME!

And too - I say unto them which hath ears to hear Me - ARISE and FOLLOW ME -- And where I go ye may go also -- I say - YE SHALL FOLLOW ME - and I shall bring thee into the place wherein I AM - and therein I shall place about thy shoulders My garment - the ROYAL RAIMENT - and upon thy brow I shall place My Seal - and I shall place within thy hand My Scepter - and I shall give unto thee the Power and the Authority to speak as I speak -- And I shall give unto thee Power and the Authority to do that which I do -- And ye shall sit upon the Right Hand of the Lord God - and He shall place upon thy head the Crown with which ye shall be known throughout His Kingdom as His Son - ARISEN FROM THE DEAD!

And the glad Hosanas shall ring out – HAIL! HAIL! A SON IS ARISEN HE HATH RECEIVED HIS FREEDOM AT LAST!

I say unto thee - The GLAD TIDINGS shall ring out unto all the nations of the lands - and they shall be glad! For this do I now speak unto thee - that they may Know that I Am now Come for to deliver them out of bondage ---

I say unto them - that All which believe upon Me - shall believe upon these My Words - and unto them I say - Ye shall find Me - and I shall bring thee out of bondage - and ye shall go into all the secret places of the Earth ---

Ye shall be free even as I Am free - Ye shall arise - free from the gravitation of the Earth - and free from all bondage - and free from <u>any bound</u> -- And ye shall ascend even as I did ascend unto My Father ---

I say unto thee - It is now come when many shall ascend even as I did ---

And too I say -- They shall receive of Me the Water of Life - and they shall drink deeply of the Substance of LIFE - Which is Liquid Light -- The Spoken Word made Substance - LIQUID LIGHT - made Substance ---

And when ye see One holding within Their hand a CRYSTAL GOBLET Which has within it the Sparkling Nectar of LIFE - Ye shall ask of that One - "MAY I DRINK?" ---

And when ye have drunken of this Substance ye shall step forth from thy old body of dense substance - of atomic Earthly substance - into the body of LIGHT Substance - thy CHRIST BODY - and ye shall be free forever more ---

Ye shall go into darkness no more -- Nor shall ye know suffering of any kind - in any manner - for I say unto thee - yes shall be free of the gravitation of the Earth - free from the attraction of the Moon - and ye shall go into bondage no more -

I say unto thee -- BEHOLD ME THE LORD ARISEN - AND BEHOLD ME THE SON OF GOD - THE GOD OF GLORY! For I AM the Prince of Glory! Behold Me I AM Come that ye may Know Me the Lord thy God -- For He the Father - hast sent Me in His Name that ye may be brought out of bondage and return unto Him ---

I AM thy Older Brother which has gone before thee to prepare the Way before thee -- Follow Me - and I shall lead thee out -

I AM Sananda

Recorded by Sister Thedra

Mother Eternal - "Arise as the Phoenix"

Beloved Children - My Children - which I have given birth - the birth which shall never become void - or nil - for I have created thee divinely and thou art infinite - without end – for from Me thou hast gone out and from Me thou hast been sustained -- I say thou art My fingers upon my right hand - and thou art sustained by My Breath which I breathe. By My heart beat thou art sustained -- And I say unto thee O MIGHTY ONES - thou art ME! -- While thou cannot see Me -- Neither can thy toe see thy eye -- Thy eye can see thy toe - and thy toe knows not thy head - or hand -- Yet they are thee- and ye know the suffering one for the other ---

My Children - thy longing has been great and thy wandering sad - yet ye have wandered long and far -- It is now come when ye shall return unto Me and be made Whole - for I am now prepared to bring thee in -- Thou hast willed it so - and so be it ---

Ye have called out for Light and Mercy -- It shall be given -- Now I say unto thee that Mighty shall be thy Work for it shall be as the MIGHTY OAK - and it shall withstand the tempest - and the whirlwinds for they shall not destroy thy works which shall endure -- I say unto thee - which do My Work - that I shall sustain thee - I shall be unto the all that ye need ---

Praise ye the Name of Solen Aum Solen - and give unto Him all the glory - all the praise - and then ye shall glorify Him in the Earth - and they shall see thy Light which shall radiate out into all the lands of the Earth - and therein shall I glorify thee in the place wherein I AM --- I say unto them which come into the place wherein ye are - that they shall be blest - And they shall come unopinionated - unbiased - UNopinionated - for there is thy legirons - For it is now time to lay aside thy pre-conceived ideas and thy petty theories -and seek the Truth - the Light - which shall never fail ---

Beloved ones - I say let nothing deter thee from thy progress - Make haste this day and be ye alert - Keep fast unto the laws set down for thee - be vigilant- and ask of no man his opinion - Keep thy own council and be as one which has my hand upon thee - and I shall give unto thee strength to endure ---

And the mind in Me shall be thy mind - and ye shall arise as she PHOENIX from the ash - and build anew -- And therein is My promise which I have given unto thee from the beginning of thy sojourn -- For

My love have I have not forfeited - I have not taken it away - and no man shall make void My Words - and they shall return unto Me bearing witness of My Love and My Being - So be it My testimony unto thee - - I AM thy Mother Eternal..

Recorded by Sister Thedra

Ye Shall Bless Thyself

Beloved Ones: My hand moves upon the land-upon the waters thereof; and I make my face to shine thereon--

I say unto thee- I AM thy father eternal--and I AM without beginning without end--I go not-neither do I come--I AM---I AM within the earth

I AM the solar system--systems without end have I created-- Wherein is thy limitation?

For from me hast I given unto thee BEING--I say, I limit thee not. And by my spoken word shall I deliver thee out of bondage for I have willed it so -so shall it be ---

I say unto thee I AM NOT limited yet ye shall give unto me cred for that which I AM---and ye are to obey mine laws--and ye shall bless thyself by the doing-- for this have ye been commanded to obey them- and then ye shall return unto me- and I shall accept thee so be it and Selah.

I am now prepared to give unto thee thy inheritance in full when ye have become the age of responsibility- and when ye have given unto me credit for that which I AM ---

I say unto thee, I AM thy father, and I AM responsible for MY WORDS and MY ACTIONS - and when I speak unto the I have to account unto NO man for MY WORDS- or MY LANGUAGE--- I have commanded thee to come as a little child- and as such have I received thee--and as such I speak thee---

I bless thee as a father- and I say, that I AM a good father- and I AM responsible unto thee for bringing thee forth---

Now I say unto thee- I have given unto thee one gift, "FREE-WILL" and I shall never trespass upon it--yet when ye use it, that it me be for thy return unto me, I shall be glad - and mine heart shall rejoice for long have I waited thy return---

HOLY- HOLY - is MY NAME- remember it- and keep it so---

I AM Solen Aum Solen----

Recorded by Sister Thedra

Easter Morning - Christ Speaks
Sori Sori - the Christ speaks unto thee this day: that which is Spirit sayeth unto thee; BEHOLD THAT WHICH IS SPIRIT - that which is eternal and which is pure - pure, of its purity by divine endowment of the Father's virtue made pure --

I say that Spirit is life - pure in its purity which is of God the Father by HIS VIRTUE, and by HIS NATURE - Now ye shall be unto thyself true, and declare for thyself thy freedom from bondage - thy freedom from darkness - and ye shall cleanse thyself of all preconceived concepts of the Father/Mother God - and thy source - all thy opinions; for I say unto thee, man of Earth has not conceived the fullness of HIM the Father, nor His handiworks; for he has been as one whose head is bound and he has enshrouded himself in a great mist - he is enmeshed as a fly enmeshed within the web of the spider - He has been indoctrinated through the ages - from the beginning of thy sojourn - and he has gone in and out of the flesh as a wanderer in darkness - he returns again and again- to find himself entangled within the same web - and he has played his part in the weaving - for not one stands alone in his enmeshed condition.

Yea, sad indeed, the MASS is enmeshed as the fly! I say it is INDEED sad! For not any one, stands alone - for as a people dost thou go out and as a people dost thou weave the 'web of illusion' --

And I say unto thee only thy own effort - thy own free will can free thee, for therein is thy freedom - and let it be for the good of all that ye seek thy own freedom - for therein is wisdom.

I say unto thee great and powerful are the ones now sent to bring unto thee TRUTH, LIGHT, and LIFE more fully shall ye live, greater shall be thy work, lighter thy way, and great shall be thy reward.

I say unto thee ye shall be as one free from all thy dogmas, creeds, legirons, bondage and ye shall be as ones free forever. Yet I say unto thee, this day - ye shall will it so: so be it and SELAH. Now ye shall be as one prepared to receive the greatest revelation now in this day: When ye have cast aside thy preconceived ideas of thy source, of thy GOD, of HIS SON, of thy own BEING, and of the universe about thee.

I say ye have been given false doctrines - and ye have adulterated EVEN them! Now I say unto thee, the time draweth nigh when ye shall go into the secret place of the most high living God; bare, bare, as a newborn babe - void of anything, save thy eternal 'SOUL', and it shall be clean for none other shall enter therein.

Behold thyself, this day, as a CHILD of the MOST HIGH LIVING GOD - and be ye as one clean, come as a little child, void of all thy preconceived ideas, of all thy rituals, all thy creeds and ask of HIM thy Father, thy freedom - when ye have asked as a little child in humbleness, and with a contrite heart HE shall have compassion on thee, and HE shall accept thee as HIS own, with love and compassion and He shall be unto thee the Father of love and mercy - So be it and SELAH.

I give of myself that this may be my gift unto thee this day, I am Sananda, the Nazarine, Son of God am I, sent to show thee the way - follow ye me - I AM the one gone before thee that the place be prepared for thee, it is done, I AM come that ye may return with me - Let it be so - SANANDA

Recorded by my servant, my hand made manifest - she is one with me, I am the hand, I am the mind, I am the one sent of HIM, my FATHER, that prophecy may be filled - she is my servant, which I call Thedra, and is thy benefactor, even as I am hers - remember this - as ye would that I remember thee.

I Would Speak unto Thee of Devotion

Beloved Ones: This day I would speak unto thee of devotion - devotion unto the great and mighty, all-wise giver of all- good and glorious gifts. I say unto thee, Mighty He is and ever shall be!

I speak unto thee this day as one which has gone the royal road; and I am qualified to speak as thy Older Brother, for I am, Now let it be understood, that when one is called out from among them, and they have answered the call, this set them apart from all others, from them which are yet in darkness - Now when they answer the call they are as ones set apart, for this have they been called; and when they give of themself whole-heartedly, with all their will and all their energies, they devote themself to the work at hand, they divide not themself, they give not of themself to the things of the world, neither do they run hither and yon seeking man's opinions, or favors; for I say, they MATTER NOT! Now when they, the ones called out, are so prepared for any part which is prepared for them, then they shall receive it - not until they are prepared for it - and wherein is is it written that as they are prepared so shall they receive. So be it and SELAH.

Now I say, they which are devoted unto the plan, and are found trustworthy shall be greatly rewarded, for they shall be as one which has 'earned the right' to call themselves "Teacher-Master-Sibor" or any other name - I say, by any other name they earn the right, which is their passport, they pass not through the portals of the temple of Light until they have proven themself worthy.

I say as they are prepared so shall they receive - so be it and SELAH. I say unto thee; be ye as one devoted unto thy calling - let nothing turn thee aside, and give unto the altar all thy energy - all thyself, all thy time, for this have I brought thee hence, and for this have I commanded thee "Follow Ye ME" - I go not into the place of iniquity, I go not into the dens of thievery - I go not wandering - I say I AM alert unto my part, and I am about my Fathers business, and naught else - By my hand shall ye be staid while thou dost obey my commandments - yet, I say unto thee; I sibor not fools for they are as the foolish - and they are not as yet prepared to receive that which I have kept for them so be ye as wise as the serpent, and silent as the sphinx - I AM thy Sibor and thy Brother - Sananda

Recorded by Sister Thedra

Arise from Thy Tomb

Behold: My Hand moveth upon the land - within the firmaments - they moveth upon the sea - within ALL Galaxies which I have created - yea unto the Universes which I have populated --

I say that I have populated these Universes without number - and I say I AM NOT LIMITED - I AM without limitation and I AM the ALL that is - which shall endure throughout the fullness of time --

I say unto thee - ARISE FROM THY TOMB OF DARKNESS - REACH OUT FOR THE FULLNESS OF ME - AND YE SHALL BE FILLED --

For I say - Unto ME belongs the Glory - and the foresight - for have I not known aforehand that which should come upon thee?-MY CREATION - MY HANDIWORK - Have I been found napping? I say unto thee - NAY! NOT SO! For I have reached out My Hand and I have moved it thusly - and there has appeared great and glorious demonstrations of Me - Of My Works - Yet Man of MY CREATION asks not of Me - yet they seek wisdom among themselves - and they give unto themself credit for being wise - while they torment themself with their own creation- and they will their own misfortune - they turn not unto Me for their salvation WHICH IS ME! WHICH I AM --

Yet when they torment themself enough they shall find the futility of such folly - and they shall be as made humble - and as ones which come of a contrite heart - as a little child - and therein is wisdom for I shall receive them in the fullness of My Love - and I shall bless them as none other - for I AM the giver of ALL that is GOOD and eternal - I say I AM the giver of LIFE - LIGHT - I AM and beside ME there is NO OTHER -- I AM - O

Beloved: I speak unto thee out of the fullness of time - and I say unto thee great and MIGHT is the Power of the ETERNAL FATHER SOLEN AUM SOLEN - MIGHTY is HE - Great is His Name - and MIGHTY is HIS WORD - and Precious HIS Name - PRAISE ye HIS Name --MIGHTY ONE ARISE! - take up thy crown - and sing ye the everlasting AUMS -- Power is thine - endowed unto thee by the Giver of all Great and Good gifts - yea - Life Itself - MIGHT - POWER lies within thy hand - and I say unto thee - ARISE! speak the "WORD" and ye shall be called HOLY - and HOLY art thou - I say be ye as one made Whole - walk this day with Me - and I say ye shall not stumble - neither shall ye falter - Bless this day, and remember it and give thanks it is now come-

I AM HE - Which keeps watch at thy door - I AM HE - the door-keeper - the Porter at thy gate - I AM HE - which has gone before thee that the Way be prepared before thee - walk therein with grace befitting

A CHILD of the MOST HIGH LIVING GOD -- I AM thy Older Brother -

Recorded by Sister Thedra

I Am Thy Lord Thy God

BEHOLD ME this day - and know that I AM THY LORD - THY GOD. Arise with Me - blend thy Light with MINE - that it may become as MINE and that there be Light within the world of men - that they may see it - that they may walk by it --

Let it be that they shall see that ye are ONE with ME - that ye are ME - MINE - which I have ordained into the Priesthood of Melchizedek that thou hast qualified for this Part - so be it thou hast qualified - yet I say unto thee ye wait for the time - for the opportue time when All the Gifts shall be bestowed upon thee - and for this dost thou wait - yet I say thy waiting shall cease - and ye shall go forth as My hand made manifest upon the Earth - and ye shall speak MY WORDS - the Words which I shall put into thy mouth and they shall fill the lands of the Earth and they shall bless all which do hear them for they shall be filled with Wisdom and Power --

And that Power shall lift them from their slumber - and from the dead shall they be lifted - yea - I say unto thee they shall be blest as only I can bless them - and My Arm is not shortened --

For I AM the ALL WISE - ALL POWERFUL GOD - which has brought them forth - yea - I have given unto them Life - and I have endowed unto them LIFE and FREE WILL - yet they go their own willful way and they use not these gifts to glorify themself in ME --

I say they are as thorns in my side - for they know Me not - these MINE CHILDREN - which I have sent out from ME - as rays of MINE OWN SELF have I projected them into the Cosmos - yea- throughout the Cosmos have I sent them forth - and now - they -mine children - have turned their face from ME - their Father!

Now I speak unto them as such - THERE SHALL COME WITHIN THE TIME WHICH IS NEAR - A DAY OF ACCOUNTING - and that day shall be a GREAT DAY - which has long been prophesied - and this shall be the final judgement - for I say the Earth shall no longer be a cradle for the sleepers - and they shall be belched out - for they shall No Longer pollute the elements of the Earth - and defile Her! for She too shall be delivered up from Her travail - for She has Now received the HOLY ONE - and with Him His Host of Angels - and the MIGHTY ONES draweth even closer - nigh unto the Earth - yea they are within the Earth as men of flesh - as guardians of TRUTH and JUSTICE - and I say they are CLOSE! CLOSE!

Nigh unto thee through birth of flesh - and *also* through NY SPOKEN WORD which is made manifest - these have not taken birth from the womb of woman - neither have they had their memory blanked from them. Now let it be said that in this day I shall raise up Mine Children from the lowly and the oppressed - and I shall exalt them above the wise! And they - the "wise" shall be humbled and brought low - yes unto the end shall I work MY STRANGE ACT!

Ye which know Me not call My "STRANGE ACT" impossible??

I say unto them: "YE FOOLISH ONES!" see My hand move - see Me - and take heed of My words - for My "ACTS" shall be strange unto thee - for none of thee which do sit in high places and call themself 'wise' can - nor shall ye perform such as I shall!

I say I am not mocked! and woe unto any man which doth usurp My Power and pilfer MY WORKS - and misuse the energy which I allot them I say such is blasphemy - and I am NOT of a MIND to be unto them a second - for I AM the First - and the Last! and all inclusive!

I AM the Alpha and the Omega -Cause of thy BEING - I AM SOLEN AUM SOLEN.

- - - - - - -

Beloved - let it be recorded as of old - that My Prophets have been spat upon - and seized by the neck - and cast into prison - martyred and given the freedom of the physical body - yet I say unto thee - this shall end! for I say I shall end it! No longer shall I stand and see the servants of the Father which He has given the Greater Part slain for 'their wanton (rebelliousness) and I say that it shall end NOW! For this have we called Council - I say We the Council of Twelve have called Council that it be finished - and too - I say that My Prophets shall be honored above the greatest of them which doth sit in high places and scorn My servants - My Brothers Whom hast received the gift of prophecy - Now I say there are none so foolish as the ones which think themself wise - and they shall be faced with their foolishness - so be it and Selah - Now I say that they shall be brought low - and My prophets shall be exalted above them - and it shall be for the good of all mankind - that they shall be brought low - for therein is wisdom - for by the Law they shall learn that there are none so foolish as the ones which "think" themself wise.

NOW I say I shall raise up My prophets in the Name of the Most High Living GOD - and they shall be exalted above the WISEST of them which 'think' themself wise - So be it and Selah - My hand moveth and I am not alone in this - for MY DAY is come - and I bring with Me a legion of Light-bearers - And I say unto thee: I shall prepare the just and the righteousness - and I shall give unto them gifts which they have forgotten - and I shall bless them as none other - and I shall touch them and quicken them - and they shall come alive - and they shall have their leg-irons cut away - and they shall be forever free - I say MIGHTY is the Arm of the Father which has sent Me - and He has endowed unto Me HIS Estate _ and I say unto thee - that ye may receive of ME as I have received or HIM - So be it MY DIVINE RIGHT to endow thee with Mine Gifts - which are Mine - by Divine Inheritance - so be it that ye have proven thyself trust-worthy - and I Am glad - Was it not said that as ye are prepared so shall ye receive? So be it and Selah. I Am glad this day is come - I Am thy Brother - and thy Sibor

Sananda -

Recorded by Sister Thedra

Creeds and Dogmas - Solen Aum Solen

Behold ME--My Children- I come unto thee as thy Father Solen Aum Solen--I give unto thee freely that ye may know me- even as I know thee for this do I speak unto thee in language which thou dost comprehend-yet My Children, I say unto thee: ye are as babes in swaddling clothes for ye do not comprehend the fullness of me- the plan which I have for thee- for I AM a father beyond thy present limitation; I limit thee NOT- yet ye have imposed upon thyself great and hazardous limitations-- thou hast forged for thyself many legirons, and thou hast been bound thereby.

NOW I say unto thee cast away thy leg-irons free thyself from all bondage and return unto me- for thou dost not come unto me bound by thy dogmas- and thy creeds- thy fortunes of earth; for NOT ONE of MINE shall be better by thy creeds- thy dogmas- thy own preconceived ideas of ME---

And I say unto thee; the lowly shall be exalted above the highest of them who doth sit in the seat of judgment and pronounce judgment - unrighteous judgment upon then---

Be ye as ones wise, and turn unto me thy father and ask thy freedom from bondage and I shall send a legion unto thee that ye may be unbound--so be it MY WILL that none perish in darkness- for this have I sent Mine Sons unto the world of darkness that ye may have light---

I say, lift up thine eyes unto the heavens from whence ye went out praise ye this day- give thanks it is come- for this have I opened up this seal- and therein ye shall read and perceive MY WILL, and it shall be done, in earth as it is in heaven, so be it I AM

SOLEN AUM SOLEN.

Recorded by Sister Thedra

PORTIONS OF THE SIBORS

The Eternal Mother

Sarah speaking:-

Beloved of my bosom - beloved of my being - of my heart: I have given myself that ye might be - I have given unto thee expression - I have given unto thee the will to be as one prepared to return unto the place of thy going out ---

I have waited thy return - I have longed for thy return -- I have held thee fast in the hours of thy unknowing - I have given unto thee words which have astonished thee when they proceeded from thy lips -- I have manifested before thee in many forms - I have given unto thee strength to overcome thy weakness ---

I have put within thy hand mine - I have led thee thru the hours of despair -- I have gone into the depths with thee - I have climbed the summits with thee -- I have gone into the dragon's den that ye might be blest of me - I have gone into the temples of many a planet with thee that ye might have light - I have been unto thee thy guiding light ---

I have brot thee into this place wherein ye shall be as my hand made manifest unto them - and ye shall say unto them as I would say - that "There shall be the two - one shall be taken and the other left - many are called and few are chosen"-- So be it and Selah -- I say they which are chosen - are chosen for their fitness and for their ability to learn -- I say - they which are of a mind to learn shall be as ones prepared for the greater part ---

Yet it is necessary to put aside the old and put on the new - I say that the old shall be put off and the new shall be put on -- Too I say - as ye are prepared so shall ye receive - such is the law -- I say that when ye come unto the altar which the Father has caused to be set up - as a little child and asked for light - unopinionated and with contrite heart - ye shall be answered -- Ye shall ask of Him thy freedom from bondage and He shall hear thee and answer thee -- So be it and Selah -- I say that none shall tell Him what He shall do - and he which says that which the Father shall do is the greatest of fools - I say they are as ones bound in darkness - they know not - I say they are the unknowing ones ---

Be ye as one which can come unto this altar clean of hands and of heart - and ye shall be lifted up -- So be it I come that they may all be brot out of bondage -- So be it and Selah ---

I am thy Mother Eternal

          Recorded by Sister Thedra of the Emerald Cross

Berea-Sanat Kumara... Spouse Eternal

Berea speaking: - Be ye as my hand made manifest - and say unto them as I would say - that I am one with Sanat Kumara as his right hand - as his one and only spouse eternal -- I am eternally wed with him - I am not separated from him - and I am not to be separated from him ---

I am known by other names - yet I speak unto thee as Berea for it is given unto me to be Berea - and that is another story-- I come that they may know me - and I am now prepared to speak at length on many subjects which shall enlighten them - and they shall profit thereby ---

I say I shall speak on many subjects at length in the time which is near and it shall profit them -- So be it and Selah -- I say ye shall be as my hand made manifest unto them - for ye have been unto me as one prepared for this part and I find thee acceptable ---

So be it I am glad -- They shall be as ones blest by me and of me - Now ye shall say unto them - that there shall be a gathering in - and they shall be brot together as the brides and bridegrooms - they shall return unto their places of abode - unto the place from which they went out -- I say they which are brot together for the fulfillment of the covenant shall be brot in as the brides and bridegrooms ---

So be it there shall be many and the joy shall abound within the place wherein I am - for I say they shall be brot in as a part of the host for they shall be part of the great army which shall go out with the King of Glory ---

He shall be as one which is to be born of woman - and the brides and bridegrooms shall make up the great part of the host which shall attend him -- So be it and Selah -- I shall speak of this again -- So be it and Salah ---

I am Berea - Sister of the Emerald Cross

"Brides – Bridegrooms"

Berea speaking:-

Beloved of our being: Be ye blest this day -- I come as Berea - for I speak for the two which is one - never to be separated -- And I say unto thee - that in the time which is now at hand - that many shall be united thru the first law - the law of "completeness"- the law of "oneness" - the law of "perfection" ---

I say unto thee - that they might have these my words - that it is now come when many shall be brot in and united as the brides and bridegrooms of God the Father -- I say that it is now come when these things shall be accomplished - which have been referred to in thy holy writ -- They have not been understood by the ones which have placed their own interpretation upon them ---

I say it is now come when these things shall be common knowledge and ye shall be given the comprehension which is of the initiate -- I say that ye shall now come to know the meaning of these things which have been so maltreated by the uninitiated---

I say I shall speak with thee on many subjects - and this one is dear unto my heart - for I see so much unreal love and sorrow and suffering because of thy unknowing -- I say it is now come when great light shall be shed upon the hitherto mysteries of life upon the planet Earth -- I say that great light shall be shed upon the 'hitherto' mysteries - and there shall be no more mystery concerning these things ---

I say that I see and know that which causes all thy sorrows and suffering - and they are as nothing when the cause is understood - and when ye do work with the law which is given unto thee from the beginning -- So be it that I speak unto all mankind at this time that there might be peace among thee ---

I say -- from the beginning of thy going out from the Father Mother God (dual in principle) that ye were made in Their Likeness and in Their "Image" - They "imaged" thee and they sent thee forth as <u>one</u> -

as one made perfect and complete -- I say ye were as one - completed in perfect oneness as man - as <u>man</u>ifestation of God the Parent - Mother-

I say - when ye divided thyself - ye did it of thy own free will - ye gave unto the Father thy vow that ye should return unto Him and take up thy sword and thy shield ---

Let this not be misunderstood by the ones which think themself wise -- I say thy sword and thy shield is the armor of God the Father - the Power - the Truth - the Law - the understanding of the law - the fulfilling of the law - and the will to do - I say that the fulfilling of the law is the will of God ---

And when ye have the will to follow within the law set before thee from this day forth ye shall be within the protection - and under the guidance of the Great "White Star" - the Order of Melchizedek - and the Order of the Emerald Cross---

I say unto thee: These are not Orders of man nor of Earth - these Orders are of divine origin - and are composed of the Federations of many systems and galaxies thruout the Cosmos ---

I come unto thee thru the Order of the Emerald Cross -- I speak unto thee as Berea and Sanat Kumara - I am his female counterpart - I am one eternally wed with him and I am glad -- So be it and Selah ---

Berea

Recorded by Sister Thedra of the Emerald Cross

Berea - Twin Ray

Berea speaking unto thee that they might have these my words -- I say unto them which are yet bound in the world of men - that there are none so foolish as the ones which think themself wise - and none so sad as he who betrays himself or his trust ---

It is indeed a great truth - and when this lesson is learned ye are ready to begin thy work - thy preparation for the greater part - so be it the first lesson ye shall learn -- I say - when the initiate begins his work he learns this lesson - he learns that there are greater things in the universe than he has dreamed of ---

So be it he walks in the way set before him - with the hand in his Sibors' - his head high - his eye single - and his mind set upon his goal He is not divided - he meditates upon the laws set before him - he walks as tho he had a crown upon his head - and he walks not in the footsteps of the transgressor -- He gives unto his Benefactors credit for knowing that which they say and do - he gives unto the Father all the credit for his being - yet he gives unto his Benefactors credit for his well-being.

He has won the first battle when he reaches the first rung of the ladder - and I say there are many -- He which is opinionated shall be among the wanton and among the unlearned - for thy opinions shall be as tacks in thy shoes ---

It is said: "Come as a little child and I shall give unto thee water which ye know not of"-- So be it and Selah -- I say they shall come as a little child - and they shall bring with them nothing! - nothing -- They shall find all their inheritance intact which has been kept for them -- So be it and Selah---

I say - when it is come that they have finished their mission within the Earth and have returned victorious - they shall be united with - and unto their ray which has waited - and they shall be in twain no more - forever shall they be united - and therein is another story ---

I shall speak with thee at length upon that - so be it shall wait ---

I am thy Sister and thy Sibor - Berea

Recorded by Sister Thedra of the Emerald Cross

Stephani Speaking

Now I say unto thee which are my channels, which are my messengers, that it is now come when ye shall be brought together for that which shall be given unto thee to do. Now be ye alert, for one shall pass over thee and he shall observe thee in the places wherein ye shall be and ye have been told that we do observe thee and see thee as ones bound in darkness.

Ye are now passing through trials and tribulations and I say it is only the beginning, for there shall be dark and trying days ahead and ye shall stand as the ROCK, for I say the Temple shall be built upon a ROCK - I say the cornerstone has been laid for this temple within the place wherein ye are. Now I say unto thee, Thedra, ye shall go from these which now sit with thee and ye shall return unto them and be unto them my hands made manifest and ye shall bring them out from the place wherein they shall find comfort and safety. I shall lead them into a place of safety wherein they shall find comfort.

Now let it be said that many shall be discomforted before the great day of sorrow - such is our part to lessen the sorrow- yet I say they shall prepare themself that they may be delivered up - so be it that one shall be sent unto them in the name of the Father, Son and Holy Ghost, Amen and Selah. I am thy Brother Stephani.

Stephani speaking: Now was it not said that there would be a gathering in - a gathering together. And was it not done? And was it not said that one should come unto them which was prepared to receive.

I say that not one but three were present for the purpose of giving unto them that which was wise. I say each which was present upon that Holy ground was indeed blest. And I say we of the XTX stood guard as the Star Ship did stand guard upon the horizon on that night and day of Sananda's birth.

I say that the XTX did monitor and stand guard upon the horizon that night which shall live within the heart of each one which stood upon the Holy ground which has been dedicated to Truth and Justice. I say that them which stood upon the Holy ground upon that mountain which has been hallowed for many centuries shall come into the full realization of that which has been done and which shall be done shall be revealed unto them.

I say that one shall go out from that sacred Temple wherein stands a white alabaster altar upon which shall lay the "Holy Writ" recorded by thy Sister Thedra ordained of God the Father. And before that altar, One shall stand and decree for thee thy freedom from bondage. And I say unto thee which now sit within the room wherein these words are being recorded that ye shall be as ones which has My hand upon thee and ye shall be blest of Me and by Me for this do I now speak unto thee.

And I say unto thee ye shall drink of the water which flows from the heart of that mountain which wears a halo of white. I say unto thee ye shall go into the place to the north from the south shall ye go and ye shall go into the north country wherein ye shall find a place for thyself.

And ye shall therein apply thyself whole heartedly unto that which shall be given unto thee to do. And when this is accomplished ye shall be illumined. And ye shall be given much revelation whereupon ye may control the elements and wherein ye may communicate with the Hierarchy. And therein is wisdom. And now I say unto thee: ye are not alone, for I am not as blind as one which has not the fortune of the Father, for I am of the Father sent to guard and to alert and direct and to sibor them which are prepared to receive such revelation.

I say the day of revelation is come when there shall be ones prepared from among the sleepers which shall be given such laws as the world has not yet comprehended. And these which are prepared for such revelation shall be as ones on whose shoulders rests the world's salvation. I say we shall not stand by and see our work go for naught.

I say the day is swiftly coming when we shall step in and we shall lift up the humble and the meek and make of them masters of the elements. And we shall cause them to be as the world has not seen! I say the ones which think themself wise shall be as fools indeed! I say they shall be confounded. I say they shall drop within their tracks from sheer fright, for they shall be as ones which have betrayed themself. And they shall know that their day is finished. So be it that when ye listen without anxiety and with the peace of mind which is thy shield and buckler I shall speak unto thee and ye shall hear me. And ye shall comprehend that which I say unto thee, and ye shall be glad.

Now I say unto thee be ye mindful of thy words for I say again we do monitor thy conversations. And I too say there are no secrets, for that which is said in secret shall be revealed. Such is the power with which we work. And I say all things shall be revealed unto the initiate. So be it and Selah. I say we give unto our own the protection necessary for the work to be done. So be it and Selah. I am Stephani of the XTX. Amen and Selah.

Recorded by Sister Thedra

Father - Mother God: I, Thedra, present myself at this altar which Thou hast set up for revelation--for the good of all mankind. That I may do Thy work as Thou would have me do it. That I may be perfect in Thy sight--and a perfect channel for the revelation yet to come. That I may not error of myself in the work Thou hast given me to do.

Cause them which do come into my presence to become aware of their own divinity--their ONENESS with Thee.

Cause them to see--and to know as Thou wouldst have them. Quicken them that their cup spills over with the joy of Thy Presence. What would Thou have of me this moment? Aum Solen?

Blest are they which do ask of Me - for they shall see Me face to face. And it is now come when ye shall be given in abundance for ye have prepared thyself for this part, such is wisdom.

Be ye as one which can comprehend that which I say unto thee and ye shall be blest of Me and by Me, so be it and Selah. Now ye shall make ready thyself for within the time which is near ye shall go into the place where in ye have not been--and therein ye shall be prepared for a part which has been kept for thee and ye shall be glad, so be it and Selah.

Now were it not that ye have been given so much to do and so little time in which to do it I should leave thee unto thy own way for ye have as yet not gone the last mile--yet it is come when great is the need for such as thee--for it is but a short while that there shall be light within the SUN---

And the sun shall be blanked out for it is night time when ye shall have no light from the sun--for it shall be darkened for a period of two weeks and there shall be much suffering and great sorrow for thy gadgets which are the tools of thy earthly scientists shall fail--even as their hearts shall fail them in the day of sorrow.

I have spoken unto thee of this time---I have commanded thee to speak unto them in My Name and thou hast obeyed-- yet they heed not me not--and they call My Oracle foolish.

I say I am with thee that thou mayest go out with the authority which I have invested within thee and say unto them that they shall take heed of Me and of My Oracles.

For I have opened my mouth and I have spoken--that they may know Me--that they might turn their face homeward--that they may not know suffering.

I am a merciful Father, yet I have given them free will and I shall not take it from them--so shall they do that which they will.

Yet I WILL that they ALL return now! And that they suffer no more--yet they are as ones deaf unto My Voice.

I say I have raised thee up--I say I have raised thee up from the dead--that I may glorify Myself through thee--and for this have I revealed Myself unto them through thee.

THE SIBORS PORTIONS

Part #49

Blest of my being: Be ye prepared for that which shall be given unto thee by our blessed Sister of Light - Nada - for she has kept a part for thee - and ye shall give it unto them which await her words -- For it is the better part of wisdom that they receive that which she has for them. So be it given unto them in the name of the Father - Son and Holy Ghost.---

Sister Nada

Blessed Sister of the Emerald Cross: Be ye blest of my being - and of my presence -- For I have given unto thee that which is given unto me of the Father - Son and Holy Ghost -- So be it and Beleis -- I am prepared to receive thee into the place wherein I am - and ye shall be glad to enter into my place of abode -- So be it and Selah --

I am come at this time that they shall be given those words -- And as for that - many have said them - yet it is given unto me of the Father to say them again - and many more shall repeat them again and again - For it is given unto some to hear and to some to wait - and these are for them which have waited - and may they heed and profit therefrom --

I am giving unto thee power and authority to say unto them that which has been given unto me of the Father - and as He gives unto me I shall give unto thee -- And as ye receive of me ye shall give unto them and they shall not say it is thy own saying - and of thy own imagination. For it is said that the Master Sananda our blessed Director (and of the grand estate which is willed unto Him of the Father - which is called "The Son of God") stands watch that none enter thy port without His permission - that He keeps thy channel pure - that He may enter in -- And for that have I been given permission to enter thy port - for it is but one of His parts that He keeps thy port clean and pure ---

And for that have we worked that ye may be prepared to receive us -- And now that ye are prepared - we shall use thee in the way which the Father shall deem wise -- And so be ye prepared that ye may receive of the Father - Son and Holy Ghost -- So be it and Beleis --

I am come as is also our blessed Master and Director Sananda - that ye may receive the "Greater Part" - and ye shall receive thy new name and thy new body - and ye shall know as we know -- Ye shall go and come as we -- Ye shall be as the ones which have free communication with the Father -- Ye shall give unto them which are bound within the world of men as we give unto thee -- For it is given unto us to prepare thee for the Inner Temple - and ye shall prepare them even as we have been prepared by them which have gone before us ---

And ye shall pass among them and ye shall seek out them which are prepared to receive - and ye shall put upon their foreheads a mark - and ye shall give unto them that which shall be given unto thee for them and ye shall receive thy own reward -- For ye shall be as one commissioned to bring them in -- And so be it and Selah ---

Now that it is said unto them that they shall be prepared to receive thee in the name of the Father - Son and Holy Ghost - so shall they heed these words which are given unto them in love - mercy and wisdom -- And they shall be glad for their preparation - and for their knowing -- So be it and Selah ---

I am come - as the Father has sent me - that they may receive of His Grace thru thee -- So be it and Selah --

I am thy Sister Nada - of the Emerald Cross ---

* * *

The Blessed Director - Sananda

Blest of my being: I have given unto thee that which has been thy passport into the Inner Temple -- And as I have come unto thee - and as ye have received me I shall give unto thee that which is given unto me of the Father - Son and Holy Ghost - for it is given unto me to be the Director of the New Dispensation - and for that am I prepared ---

In the days of my youth in the city of Jerusalem - and of Egypt - I was received into a certain temple wherein they taught the laws of Moses - and wherein they denied the law which had been given unto us of the dispensation of that day -- They gave no credence unto the Father for their being - they gave unto their Benefactors no recognition --

So be it that the same ones which stood as my disciples which received of my instructions - which were given unto me of the Father - are in the "world of flesh and bone" today -- For it is given unto us to bring into fruit that which was begun then - and that which has laid dormant within the embryo - and which shall now come into full maturity ---

For it has been given unto me to renew my covenant with them which are as yet dead unto that which is given unto them of the Father. They have wandered thru the valleys and thru the darkness wherein there was but little light - and it has faded upon their altars - and nothing is left save the skeletons of their bygone martyrs - and the parts which have been reportioned and retold until they are scarcely recognized ---

And now there shall be a great house cleaning - for their bloody saints shall be removed from their altars -- Their idols of wood and brass shall be replaced by flesh and bone -- And the words spoken from their pulpits shall be those of the Father - for He has willed it that all shall come to know that which is their inheritance - and that which is willed unto them of Him --

They shall no longer wander in darkness! They shall know - and it shall be given unto them to walk in the Light of the Christ - for they shall no longer be bound by the black dragon -- And they shall not be as ones led by the blind! - for they shall be their own saviors - and they shall be unto themself true ---

They shall have no "blood sacrifice" - and they shall be as ones delivered out of darkness -- For it shall be given unto many to walk and talk with them which are sent out from the Father - that this new dispensation may come into its fullness -- And so be it and Selah---

I am the Man of Galilee - which speaketh unto thee - and it shall profit thee to hear that which I have said unto thee - for I am come that my covenant may be fulfilled - and that ye may be brot out of darkness So be it and Beleis -- Sananda - the Son of God the Father - and whom ye have called Jesus of Nazareth ---

Bernard

Blessed Sister of the Emerald Cross: Be ye blest of my presence and of my being - for I am come unto thee as our blessed Director and faster has come - that they may know wherein they are staid -- It is given unto me to be one of those who was His disciple - and He has given unto me permission to come unto thee for this part - as it shall be given unto us to sit in council with Him in the secret place of His abode - and to learn of Him - and from Him - the part which we shall have within the new plan and the new dispensation

And we shall be given our parts according to our preparation -- It has been given unto me to go into the secret places wherein ye shall go and to see the wonders thereof -- I have stood with tears streaming down my face in awe and gratitude - for the privilege of beholding such beauty -- I have sat upon a solid golden stone which would stagger thy imagination! I have held within my hands condensed light rays weighing many carats - and I have given unto the Father praise ---

And for the very privilege of being within these places have I pledged myself unto the Father - for His work which shall be done in me - and by me - and thru me -- And I shall not falter - nor shall I fail - for it is given unto me of the Father that which He has willed unto me I have received my Sonship - and I have received my new body and my new name -- And it shall be given unto thee to remember me - as I have remembered thee --

For it was given unto us to be with our beloved Master and Director in the days of His early journeys thruout the "Holy Land" - which has become the "unholy land" - And so shall it again be cleansed and purified - and we shall have our part in that plan -- So be it and Selah - I am thy Brother and thy Sibor - Bernard - of the Emerald Cross - and of the School of the Seven Rays ---

* * *

Beran

Blessed Sister of the Emerald Cross: Be ye blest of my presence and of my being -- For it is given unto me to come unto thee from out of the Inner Temple - and wherein I have kept a place for thee -- For from the place wherein I am - shall ye go out - and ye shall be received into the world of men - as we which shall go out when the hour strikes -- For the Father has so willed it that there shall be many sent-- And they which are so minded may be prepared to enter into the place wherein I am ---

And it shall be the better part of wisdom to prepare thyself -- For it is given unto us to bring into fruit the new plan which has been revealed unto us - and which shall be revealed unto them which are so prepared Now ye shall be given thy new part - and ye shall return unto them - as the hands of the Father and Mother made manifest unto them -- And they shall receive thee in His name - and they shall be unto themself true -- And they shall receive thee in love and honor -- So be it and Beleis ---

I am thy Brother and servant in the Light of the Christ - and in the Order of the Emerald Cross - Beran - of the Inner Temple ---

Blest of my being: Be ye at peace and poise - and ye shall receive of the Father - Son and Holy Ghost -- So be it and Beleis -- Be ye prepared to receive that which shall be given unto thee of the blessed Brother of Light - Maroni - for he has a part for them - and it shall be given unto them with the three which is before this - and they shall be sent out as one -- So be it that they shall know that which goes on about them - which has hitherto been secret ---

Now it is the day of revelation - and they which are so prepared may enter into the council chambers - and see and know that which has yet to be revealed unto the unprepared -- And so be it and Beleis ---

* * *

Maroni

Beloved Sister of the Emerald Cross: Be ye blest of my presence and of my being -- For I am come that ye may be brot into the Inner Temple and for that are ye prepared - for ye have given of thyself that others may receive -- Ye have been unto thyself true-- Ye have given unto them that which has been given unto thee for them-- Ye have not given of thy own glory -- Ye have been unto them that which the Father would have thee be -- Ye have not raised thy voice in self defense -- Ye have given unto them of thy love - and labor - and ye have asked naught from them -- Ye have gone the long way to bless them - and ye shall be given thy reward - for them which giveth in secret shall be rewarded openly. So be it the law - and so shall it be ---

And now the time is come when ye shall return unto them - and ye shall receive that which ye shall be given for them -- And they shall receive thee in love and honor - for the decree has gone out that they shall be prepared to receive thee --So be it and Beleis -- I am thy Sibor and Brother of the Inner Temple - and of the Emerald Cross - and of the Order of the Seven Rays -- So be it and Selah -- Maroni ---

Recorded by Sister Thedra

Part #50

Blest of my being: Be ye at peace and poise - and ye shall receive of the Father - Son and Holy Ghost -- So be it and Beleis -- Be ye prepared to receive that which is prepared for thee by our blessed one which has come out of the silence that they may know wherein they are staid -- And so be it and Selah ---

Return unto the altar within the hour and ye shall receive -- Be ye as the hands of one made manifest unto them -- For it is given unto him of the Father - that which he shall give unto thee -- So be it and Beleis.

Blest of my being: I am come unto thee that ye may know me -- I am he which is responsible for thy comfort -- I have given unto the Earth light and warmth - and I have given unto the Earth energy - and that which has sustained life thereon - and therein ---

For it is given unto me to be Tor - and my pointer is Tau - and we are "One" - yet we are two -- Sons of the Father are we - and we were sent out from Him - as part of Him - and equal unto Him - for He has given of Himself that we may have our being within Him -- He has given of Himself that ye - too - may have thy being within Him -- And ye have not remembered thy being --

Yet we have not separated ourself from Him -- Yet we remember thee which have separated thyself -- We have gone the long way to bless thee - for it is given unto Tau to be the source of light and energy for thy solar system -- And unto me - Tor - to be the director of the light and energy -- I direct it and channel it into the various parts - into various channels - and into the minds which are prepared to receive of the Source - which is the Fountain from which all thy knowledge of thy being reaches thee of the Earth -- And ye have not comprehended that of which I speak - for it is beyond thy present comprehension ---

Ye have but to ask and to apply thyself - and for that ye shall be greatly rewarded -- Such is my part to channel the energy which is pure and unadulterated - unto them which have prepared themself -- For it is the part of thine to prepare thyself to receive that which we are prepared to direct unto thee -- That energy is that which has been returned unto Tau - and that which has been purified - cleansed - and redirected back into the Earth and Her children ---

For it is said that we are responsible for thy well-being - and rightfully so - for were it not for the parts which we have been given of the Father - ye would have perished long ago -- For ye have been given unto mis-qualifying the energy which is directed unto thee-- Ye have been misusing it - and it has become that which has taken the form of the "black dragon"-- And now it is turned upon thee - and ye are tormented by him -- And it is given unto me - Tor - to remove him - and to recover that energy - and to Tau - to purify it - and unto me to re-channel it into the Earth and its inhabitants ---

And so be it that ye shall be given as ye are prepared to receive -- For it is come that they which are not prepared to receive of the new energy - that is the freshly purified energy - shall be removed by natural law - and they shall be put into a place of their own environment ---

And they which are prepared to receive shall become one with it - and they shall come into their Sonship which is given unto them of the Father -- And they shall see the Light of the Christ and walk therein -- For it is so decreed that the Earth shall be a planet for gods - and the

Sons of God the Father shall inherit it as their place of abode -- And for that is She - the Earth - being prepared -- And the Sons of God the Father are being prepared to receive their Sonship - which is their inheritance - and which has been willed unto them of the Father ---

And now it is come when we - Tor and Tau - shall bring them which are prepared into our place of abode - and we shall direct them in the use of this purified energy - and in the alchemy of transmuting that which has been mis-qualified - that which has been misused by man --

And they which are so prepared shall be given that which shall serve them well - for they shall be the ones which shall go and come freely between planets - and they shall command that which they will and it shall appear! They shall be co-creators with the Father - and they shall create like unto Him -- And for this are ye being prepared -- So be it and Selah -- I am thy Benefactor - and thy Sibor - Tor - of the Emerald Cross ---

Blest of my being: Be ye prepared to receive that which shall be given unto thee of the Blessed Benefactor - Tau - and that which he has prepared for them -- And so be it given in the Name of the Father - Son and Holy Ghost -- And so be it and Beleis ---

Blest of my being: Be ye blest of my presence -- I am he which is known as Tau - and ye have not remembered me - yet ye knew me well before ye separated thyself from me - and from the Father - before ye went out into darkness - and before ye forgot thy Source -- And now again ye shall remember thy oneness of being - and ye shall return unto the Father - and ye shall be unto Him the glory of His heart ---

For ye have now reached the age of accountability - and ye shall be told that which has hitherto been kept for thee for this day -- Now it is come that they which are so prepared may be brot into my place of abode - and they shall be trained in the alchemy of transmuting the misused - the malpresent energy - and they shall cleanse and purify it and recondition it according to the laws of love and harmony ---

They shall be given instructions in the laws of the Losoloes - and they shall become co-creators with the Father - for He has willed it so. And were it not so I would not tell thee -- Now ye shall be given unto as ye are prepared to receive - and as ye are prepared so shall ye receive. Be ye blest which are prepared - and sad shall ye be which are not - for ye shall be put into a place wherein ye may wait until ye are prepared. So be it and Selah ---

I am thy Benefactor and Sibor - Tau - of the Temple of Tau - and of the Emerald Cross -- So be it and Selah ---

Blest of my being: Be ye prepared for that which shall be given unto thee in the Name of the Father - Son and Holy Ghost -- So be it and Beleis -- I am come unto thee from out of the Temple of Tau - and I am one with the Father - for I have not separated myself from Him -- And I bring unto thee a plan which is fashioned for thy own deliverance out of bondage - wherein ye may be free - even as we are free in the Light of the Christ - which ye know not! - and which ye shall come to know.

Ye speak lightly but unknowingly of the Christ -- Ye shall be made to see the Light and to comprehend that which is the Christ - and for that are ye being prepared -- And so be it and Selah ---

I am one which has revealed myself unto thee for that purpose -- And for them so prepared - they shall receive new bodies and new names - and they shall not taste of death - nor shall they know more suffering and sorrow -- And so be it that all may partake of this plan - for it is given unto thee as thy inheritance - and of the love and mercy of the Father -- So be it the better part of wisdom to prepare thyself - and ye shall be blest of the Father - Son and Holy Ghost -- So be it and Selah ---

I am one which comes unto thee from out of the Corona of the Sun and which is known as Coroni - and which ye shall come to know as one of thy Benefactors and Sibors -- So be it and Selah ---

Blest of my being and of my presence: For I am come unto thee that ye may receive of the Father - Son and Holy Ghost -- So be it and Selah.

I am one from out of the Temple of Tau - for it is given unto me to be one of thy Benefactors - and one which has given of myself that ye may not perish -- I have given unto thee strength - and unto thee of my love and wisdom that ye may find thy way home - and unto thy Source from which ye have gone out -- So be it that ye may be prepared to receive in greater capacity and of the greater part ---

And for that have I revealed myself unto thee -- I am one of many which have gone the long way to bless thee - for I have watched thee and I have recorded thy progress - and I have measured thy strength and thy endurance - and I have given unto thee that which should serve to strengthen thee ---

And now that ye have reached the day of the new age - and ye should be to the age of accountability - ye shall be given of greater substance -- And for them which cannot partake of it - shall be as ones which choke on their own saliva -- For it is portioned out unto thee as ye have willed -- And so be it and Selah ---

I am thy Brother and Benefactor - of the Temple of Tau - and of the Emerald Cross - Coroneu ---

Recorded by Sister Thedra

Part #51

Blest of my being: Be ye at peace and poise - and ye shall receive of the Father - Son and Holy Ghost -- So be it and Beleis ---

Now ye shall be prepared to receive that which is prepared for thee by the blessed Brother of Light - Boran - for He has a part for them - and it shall be given unto them in the Name of the Father - Son and Holy Ghost -- So be it and Beleis ---

Boran

Blest of my being: Be ye blest of my presence and of my being-- For I am come unto thee that ye may be brot into the place wherein I am -- And ye shall be given that which shall serve thee well! For ye shall be given that which has been prepared for thee -- And ye shall be glad for thy preparation - for long have we waited thy coming -- And now that it is come that ye shall be brot into this place - shall we not be glad? - for ye have prepared thyself for this day -- And ye have given of thyself unto the Father and that which He has given unto thee to do -- So be it that ye shall be brot into the place wherein He is - and ye shall receive thy inheritance in full -- So be it and Selah ---

I am come from out of the Inner Temple that they may know me - and for that have I waited -- For it is given unto me to be one of the Lords of the Inner Temple - one of the Kumaras - the Keepers of the Flame - wherein we have watched and waited for the day when we might come unto thee and sponsor thee - that ye may be brot into the "Federation of Brotherhoods" which make of all men brothers - and wherein ye shall receive as we receive --

And wherein ye shall know as we know - and wherein ye may have free concourse into the places which are within the ports of other planets - and other spheres -- So be it that ye shall be prepared to receive that which is thy inheritance ---

For it is not the will of the Father that ye be Earth-bound - and that ye wander in darkness! For it is given unto all that they know freedom and that they be given their inheritance which is fortuned unto us of the Realms of Light -- We are free to go and come at will -- We are not bound even within the galaxy - for we can pass freely - and we can go and come into the Earth at will --

And so do we - for many are sent that walk among thee as fellow beings -- For it is but the plan of the Father that ye come to know that ye are not alone - and that ye are sponsored by them of higher realms -- And sad indeed would ye be if it were not so! - for ye should destroy thyself - and for that have we kept close watch ----

And so be it that we shall bring out them which are prepared - and they shall be taught the laws of the Losoloes - and returned as our ambassadors -- And ye shall be prepared to receive them in the Name of the Father - Son and Holy Ghost -- So be it and Selah -- I am thy Older Brother and Benefactor and Sibor - Boran - of the Emerald Cross

Blest of my being: Be ye prepared to receive that which is prepared for thee by our beloved Sister of Light - Sarea - which is the One and only Sister within the Flame Temple -- She is Co-guardian of the Flame in the temple with the blessed Brothers Bor and Boran - and the others which as yet have not revealed themself - and for that do ye wait -- So be it given unto thee - that they which are prepared may receive of them and be it-such as shall profit them -- So be it and Beleis ---

Sarea

Blessed Sister of the Emerald Cross: Be ye blest of my being - and of my presence - for I am come unto thee from out of the Inner Temple wherein we attend the Flame upon the altar - whereupon burns the "Eternal Light" which is part of thy own pulse beat - and wherein is registered thy progress - and wherein is thy portion which has been kept for thee -- Ye have no conception of the fullness of the inheritance - and of the greatness of the Father's plan --

For it is given unto us to be thy guardians - and we have an accurate account of thy embodiments since ye began thy travels within the Earth how long ye were in the astral planes - and how long ye have been in thy present place wherein ye are - and what ye have accomplished to bring about thy present condition - and what ye have been given to do that ye <u>have</u> <u>not</u> <u>done</u> ---

And we which are the keepers of the Flame know that which ye are capable of - and that which ye can and will do -- For the Flame knows no past - present nor future - all is recorded therein -- And so be it that all which are so prepared may enter into the Flame Temple and read that which is recorded - for it is now come - the day of thy liberation - when ye shall behold the glory of the Father's Handiwork - and that which is fortuned unto thee of Him and by Him -- and there shall be no more mystery - no more darkness -- So be it thy inheritance to know as we know - and to receive as we receive -- So be it and Beleis ---

For it is given unto me to know them which are prepared to enter into the Flame Temple - and I am prepared to receive them -- So be it and Selah -- I am thy Sister of the Flame Temple wherein ye may go which are so prepared - and of the Emerald Cross -- and of the Temple of Tau - Sarea ---

* * *

Blest of my being: Be ye prepared to receive that which is given unto thee in the Name of the Father - Son and Holy Ghost by our blessed Brother of Light - Sanat Kumara - and it shall be given unto them which are prepared to receive of Him. - and that which He has kept for them So be it and Beleis ---

Sanat Kumara

Blessed Sister of the Emerald Cross: Be ye at peace and poise - for I am come unto thee as thy blessed Director and Master - Sananda - that ye may receive thy "Sonship" - and that ye may return unto the Father and Mother and for that have many revealed themself unto thee. So be it that there shall be many from my place of abode come unto thee - and they shall be unto thee that which the Father would have them be -- They shall be given the power to bring thee into the place wherein we are - and they shall be given power and dominion over the elements - and the fullness of the Earth! ---

And they shall come unto thee in the name of the Father - Son and Holy Ghost -- They shall seek thee out and they shall prepare thee to pass thru the veil of Maya - and ye shall know no death - nor suffering nor shall ye know more darkness -- For it shall be given unto thee to receive thy sonship - and therein is freedom and mastery --

And ye shall be given as ye are prepared to receive -- It is given unto me to be one of thy Benefactors and one of thy Sibors -- And now ye shall come to know me - for I shall come unto thee many times - and ye shall be given as ye are able to comprehend -- So be it and Beleis

I am come from out of the Inner Temple wherein is our blessed Brother - Bor - and them which have yet not revealed themself -- And ye shall come to know us as ye know each other - for it is now come that ye shall be brot out of the Earth - and ye shall no longer be bound within it -- So be it and Selah -- I am thy Brother of the Inner Temple - and of the Temple of Tau - and Osiris - and of the Emerald Cross - and of the Brotherhood of The Seven Rays -- Sanat Kumara

* * *

Blest of my being: Be ye prepared to receive that which is prepared for them by our blessed Sister of Light - Borea - and that which She has prepared for them shall be given in the Name of the Father - Son and Holy Ghost -- So be it and Beleis ---

Borea

Blessed Sister of the Emerald Cross: Be ye at peace and poise - for I am come unto thee that ye may receive of the Father - Son and Holy Ghost -- So be it and Selah ---

I am one which has given unto thee of my love and wisdom - that ye may be prepared to enter into the place wherein I am -- And I am come unto thee from out of the Inner Temple - wherein is the blessed Brother Bor - and Boran -- I am the Sister of Bor and Boran - and there are more which shall later reveal themself - and for that shall ye wait - I am one which has given unto thee of my love and labor that ye may reach the age of accountability -- And now that ye are brot into this age ye shall receive the "Greater Part" - that which has been kept for thee. And so be it and Selah ---

I am one of the Kumaras which have been thy Sponsors and Benefactors - For in the days when thy Earth had but little light - and She stood on the brink of eternal darkness - we gave unto Her a helping hand -- We brot Her back into the place wherein She is - and we have held Her close and dear - for She has been unto us a "Child of wanton ways" - and She shall come into Her own - and She shall be as a shining orb within the firmament -- And so be it and Beleis --

I am one of many which have loved Her - and waited for the day of Her deliverance -- So be it that they - the children of the Earth - shall come to know us and the parts we have had with the Earth and the children thereof -

For in the time which is near there shall be no barriers between the Earth and the place wherein I am -- And ye shall be free to go and come and ye shall have free communication with us -- And ye shall have no need for thy so-called "scientific instruments"- for the Father has given unto thee that which is necessary for the communication - and as yet it is undeveloped -- For it has lain dormant for so long ye have forgotten it! Yet in times past it was used by them of the Atlantean priesthood --

And of the Motherland (in Pacific) they knew wherein they were staid - and they knew wherefrom they came -- And yet they were given unto idolatry - and for that did these places which had risen to so high an estate fall! For they were as ones which cut themself off from the Father - and which forgot that which He had given unto them -- They gave no credit unto Him -- They took credit for that which they had been given of Him - and they forgot that they were the sons of God - and as such - they owed Him that which they took for themself ---

So be it that they brot about their own destruction - which is the law and so be it and Selah -- Now they are again within the lands of the Earth - and they shall again face the great catastrophe which was once before their <u>own</u> heritage - that which they fortuned unto themself -- So be it that they may be the wiser and prepared - for the day is nigh upon them - when they shall again face the same disaster! - that is - they which are not prepared to be delivered beforehand --

And they which are prepared shall remember that which they were given in these ancient days - of the sinking of the Motherland - and of the Lotus - and there was the part which was torn away within the Caribbean Sea - known as "Posedon", and the part before the Posedon which was within the Black Sea - wherein are the lost "El" records - and which shall be revealed unto the children of the new age ---

It is given unto me to know these parts - for I have watched the Earth grow to maturity - and I know all the secret places therein - and all the records from Her beginning -- And so be it and Selah -- I am thy

Sister - and thy Sibor - of the Temple of Tau - and of the Temple of Osiris - and of the Emerald Cross - Borea ---

Recorded by Sister Thedra

Part #52

Sananda

Blest of My Being: Be ye at peace and poise - and ye shall receive of the Father - Son and Holy Ghost -- So be it and Beleis -----

Be ye prepared to receive that which has been kept for thee for this time - and which is for them -- For it is given unto Me to be one of them which has gone the long way to bless them - and so shall they be blest which receive Me and of that which I shall bring unto them -- For it is given unto Me to be one which they have cried about - and which they have prayed unto - and which they have begged alms for -- and what has it profited them?

Now that I have come unto them in the garment of flesh - and they have not sought Me out! - and they have not given unto Me credit for keeping My word unto them - and they even deny My being! and that I am flesh and bone -- And so shall they be awakened - for it is come that they shall know Me - and that which I say unto them shall be emblazoned upon their foreheads! For I shall not be denied! And I shall be given a hearing - and I shall be recognized for what I am --

And for that do I give unto them these words - and they shall take them for what they are worth - for I am not to be denied! - for the Father has sent Me into the Earth that they may know Me - and that they may receive Him thru Me -- And they shall be quickened - and they shall be made to hear that which I say unto them! So be it and Selah

I am come at this time that they may be delivered up - that they may not know sorrow and suffering -- Yet I know there are many which shall not receive Me - nor the Father which has sent Me - for them do I weep - for it is given unto Me to know that which is before them -- And I would that I could deliver them up - but it is not lawful - they must come of their own accord --

And so be it that they shall be called and called again! - and they shall be given every opportunity - for it is the better part of wisdom that they be alerted -- And for that shall I send my emissaries out to bring them in - even as the Father has sent Me - They shall have the same credentials as I have -- They shall receive their sonship even as I have They shall have the same power and authority as I have - and they shall be equal unto Me ---

So be it that ye shall be wise indeed to accept them in My name - and in the name of the Father which has given unto Me that which is for them -- And so be it that We which are so prepared shall pass among thee - and We shall seek out them which are prepared to receive Us -- And We shall touch thee and ye shall be quickened - and ye shall remember thy being and ye shall know the Father from which ye came out -- And ye shall be as one which shall pass the barrier without tasting death -- Ye shall be as one transformed -- Ye shall stand forth in thy glorified body made new - and ye shall go into all the places within the galaxy -- And ye shall be as one which has given unto thyself that which is thy inheritance - for ye have but to reach out and take it - for the Father has so willed it --

And I can do no more than point the way! -- I have cried aloud that ye may hear! I have cried unto the Father that ye may be made to see - I have given of Myself that ye may know Me - and I have gone the long way to bless thee -- And now it is come when We which are so prepared shall come unto thee and We shall speak with thee -- Yet We shall not reveal Ourself until ye are able to recognize US ---

So be it that ye may be alert! and that ye may recognize Us -- And for that do I speak these words which shall carry My love and blessing unto thee in the name of the Father - Son and Holy Ghost -- So be it and Beleis -- I am Sananda (Jesus - the Son of God) of the Inner Temple and of the Temple of Osiris and of the School of The Seven Rays - and of the Emerald Cross - and of the Temple of Tau -- And so be it and Selah ---

* * *

Blest of my being: Be you at peace and poise and ye shall receive of the Father - Son and Holy Ghost -- So be it and Beleis ---

And now ye shall receive as ye have not received - for it shall be given unto thee to record that which shall be given unto thee by one of thy Benefactors and Sibors - which has kept this part for this time - and it shall be given unto them and they which are so prepared may receive of him - and that which he has for them -- So be it and Beleis ---

Beran

Blessed Sister of the Emerald Cross: Be ye blest of my presence - for I am come unto thee from out of the Temple of Tau - and I have given unto thee that ye may be blest of me - and of my being -- I am come that ye may be prepared to receive of the Father - Son and Holy Ghost So be it and Selah --

I am one little known in the world of men - and for that do I now reveal myself that all may know me -- And as they know me they shall know the Father - for truly it is the day of revelation -- And ye shall see and know as we of the realms of Light know - for ye shall be one with us - And ye shall be given free passport into our place of abode -- And so be it and Selah ---

I am one of the ones which have been called the "Fingers of the Father" - for as He - we reach out into the farthest recesses of the solar system - and we draw in that which we call the "Substance of Life" - and we fashion therefrom forms which are to be used within the new age (which ye have had a foretaste of) - and of which our blessed Brother Bor has spoken --

And ye have not comprehended - for it is not given unto them which have not seen to know -- For it is beyond their comprehension that which the Earth shall become -- We which are of the Eloheim are prepared to reveal unto them which are prepared to receive - that which She the Earth - shall become -- For the forms of the birds - and the fauna are ready - and that of the flora is being prepared -- And it shall be given unto many to be present when the offering shall be presented unto the Father for His approval - and for His blessing ---

For it is our joy and our privilege to serve in this manner -- So shall we be glad when we can endow these forms with life - and set them free into the Earth which has been cleansed and purified and made ready to receive them --

And so be it that they which are so prepared may share in our joy and in our part which we shall have in forming the new Earth and the new heaven - for it shall be the garden of the solar system -- It shall bear new fruit and new birds and fauna which is not known by man of Earth -- And ye shall be given a part within the new creation if ye so prepare thyself -- And ye shall know such joy as is portioned unto us - we which have created unto the glory of the Father - for it is our part to create ---

There are none to dictate to us - for we have been sent out from the Father - as Creators - and as He has endowed us with the power to create in His likeness and in His image -- And so be it that we shall be given a new part when the Earth shall come into Her fullness and into Her new berth -- And so be it that we shall give unto the Father credit and we shall be glad for our part -- And we shall give unto Him thanks for the privilege of serving in the new part which shall be given us -- So be it and Selah ---

I am one of the seven builders of form and one of the Eloheim - and one of thy Benefactors -- So be it and Selah -- As in thy reflection so are ye within me - and as my reflection I am within the Father - and so be it I am the Father - and ye are me - and ye are the Father -- So be it that ye shall come to know thy oneness - and so be it that ye shall receive thy sonship - And so be it and Beleis -- I am thy Elder Brother of The Eloheim - Beran - which means "In the beginning" ---

* * *

Blest of my being: Be ye prepared to receive that which shall be given unto thee of our blessed Sister of Light - Sarea - for She has a part for thee which shall be given unto them in the Name of the Father - Son and Holy Ghost -- So be it and Beleis ---

Sarea

Blest of my being: Be ye blest of my presence for I am come out of the Temple of Tau that ye may receive of me - and that ye may be prepared to receive of the Father - Son and Holy Ghost --So be it and Beleis ---

It is given unto me to be one of thy Sibors and Benefactors -- And I have given of myself that ye may be brot into the place wherein I am. So be it and Selah -- I am come too - that the world of men may come to know that they are not alone - for it is given unto many from many planets to be unto thee older Brothers and Sisters - and for that do we watch Her and Her habitants -- For they have been wayward ones! And they have needed much guidance and love to bring them back into their rightful estate -- And so be it that the time is come when we can come unto them and counsel them as fellow beings ---

It is only the beginning - for as ye accept us and of our love and siboring - ye shall grow in strength and power and wisdom -- Yet nothing shall be given unto thee for conquest or for gain from others - nor for that which ye call profit from conquest --

And as ye pilfer and plunder each country and land whereupon ye have stood - ye shall be brot to account for each and every act of aggression and conquest - for it is the beginning of thy downfall -- And no man shall take from his fellow man that which he has not earned -- So shall ye learn and profit thereby - for it is given unto thee to forget from where thy bounty comes -- And ye shall be caused to remember - for in the time which is near all thy ill-gotten gain is to be swept before the winds! And ye shall stand as one naked and in despair - for ye shall be as one which has sown thistles wherein there is wheat - and ye shall be as ones which have no place to lay thy head - and ye shall be as ones which have no place to turn for comfort --

Ye shall call for help - yet ye may be as one which has thrown overboard thy lifebelt! And now I say unto thee that the day of reckoning is come! And ye shall turn from thy ways of aggression - and ye shall seek that which shall profit thee -- Ye shall call unto the Father for deliverance and strength - and ye shall be unto Him a servant and a son which has returned home ---

And ye shall give unto me credit for speaking openly unto thee - for it is now come when many shall stand before thee and proclaim the Truth which shall be unto thee thy Shield and Buckler - and ye shall profit to heed that which they say unto thee -- So be it and Beleis---

I am one of them which has waited for the time when I may say unto thee that which shall bring thee out of thy stupor and lethargy-- For indeed it is sad to see thee without comfort and without port - for ye shall be discomforted and deported! For ye cannot see that which is before thee - and it is given unto many to call unto thee that ye may be alerted! So be it and Selah -- I am thy Sister - and Sibor - of the Temple of Tau - the Emerald Cross - and of the Temple of Osiris - and of the Inner Temple - Sarea ---

* * *

Blest of my being: Be ye prepared to receive that which is prepared for thee by our blessed Brother of Light - Bor - for he has a part for them - which shall be given unto them in the Name of the Father - Son and Holy Ghost -- So be it and Beleis ---

Bor

Blessed Sister of the Emerald Cross: Be ye blest of my presence and of my being -- For it is come that ye shall be brot out of the place wherein ye are - and ye shall be prepared to be brot into the Inner Temple wherein I am -- And as I have free concourse into all the secret places wherein ye may go - ye may find me in any one of them - for I go and come as the Father gives unto me - for there is much being done between all the places wherein we work --

For it is a day of great activity thruout the Cosmos and there is great preparation - For now it is come when all the planets within thy present system are undergoing changes - and it shall be given unto us of the higher realms to assist our younger brothers ---

For it is that for which we are prepared - and so be it that we are prepared -- And now ye too are being prepared for that which shall be given unto thee to do - for ye are being groomed for a new part and a new place - and so are many which have been called and which have answered and presented themself for preparation -- I say unto thee: "Well done - thy reward shall be great!" and ye shall be glad --

And so be it and Selah -- I am given unto patience - and I shall wait for them which have said: "Oh - they are crying 'wolf!' and I shall wait and see what happens"-- Oh well - let them wait - and when the wolf approaches - see them run! Oh - little children which I love so dearly -

will ye not grow up? - and will ye not mature early! - for it is given unto me to know how small ye are - and such infants! and such frail ones!---

I am in the place wherein I can read thy records and watch thy progress - and it is given unto me to say that which I know and that which ye have recorded upon the "ether" --And ye have stood on the brink of destruction more than once - and we have drawn thee back -- And ye have slept on - unheedingly! And now we which have watched and waited are going to be <u>very</u> <u>firm</u> and direct - for ye shall either alert thyself or ye shall be "deported"--

And ye shall be put into a place wherein ye may sleep until ye awaken of thy own accord - and ye shall be as ones dead! for dead ye are!- for ye see not - neither do ye hear -- Ye are walking in circles - knowing not whither thou goest -- So be it that many shall be sent to awaken thee - and ye shall be in wise to stir thyself - for it is the day of awakening -- So be it and Beleis -- I am thy older Brother - and Sibor - Bor - of the Inner Temple - the Temple of Tau - and of Osiris - and of the Emerald Cross--

Recorded by Sister Thedra

Part #53

Blest of my being: Be ye prepared to receive that which is prepared for thee by our blessed Sister of the Temple of Tau - and that which She has for them shall be given unto them in the Name of the Father - Son and Holy Ghost -- So be it and Beleis ---

Borea

Blessed Sister of the Emerald Cross: Be ye blest of my being and of my presence -- For I am come unto thee that they may receive of me thru thee - even as ye receive of the Father thru me -- So be it and Beleis -- I am one of many which shall be given that which ye shall receive for them -- For it shall be given unto thee to pass into the place wherein I am - and ye shall be given of our love and our wisdom - and ye shall be trained in the laws of the Losoloes --

And ye shall be returned into the Earth as our emissary - for ye have earned the right to call thyself an ambassador -- For this have ye been sibored - and ye have received thy passport -- And so be it and Beleis I am given unto watching for them which may be trained and which may be acceptable unto the Sibors - and unto the Father -- And they are brot in as they are prepared - and so be it that there shall be many prepared from among them ---

And now I say unto them which are yet in the world of men: We which are thy Guardians and Sibors are watching and waiting -- And at the first signs we are at thy side and ready to be unto thee all that ye shall need -- We are prepared to give unto thee food and drink - and we are prepared to bring thee out of darkness - and to give unto thee that which shall be unto thee thy liberation -- And ye shall be glad for thy liberation! and for thy freedom from bondage -- So be it and Beleis ---

I am one which has stood guard for thee -- And now I am prepared to stand sponsor for thee that ye may pass into the higher realms of learning -- So be it and Selah -- I am come for that purpose - and I shall be rewarded when one comes into my place - for it is our only reward And so shall there be great joy and much gladness - for many shall be brot out of the Earth - and they shall be received in love and understanding -- And so be it and Selah -- Be ye as one which can comprehend that which I have said unto thee - and ye shall be given in greater measure -- And so be it ye shall come to know us - and ye shall commune freely with us - and it shall profit thee -- And so be it and Selah ---

I am thy Sister of the Inner Temple and of the Temple of Tau - Osiris - and the Emerald Cross -- So be it and Selah -- I am Borea ---

* * *

Blest of my being: Be ye prepared to receive that which shall be given unto thee by our blessed Brother of Light - Zamu - for He has kept a part for thee which shall be given unto them in the Name of the Father Son and Holy Ghost -- So be it and Beleis ---

Zamu

Blest of my being - and of my presence - my Sister of the Emerald Cross: And ye shall now receive that which I have kept for thee for this time -- It is given unto me to be one of them which has come that ye may be prepared to receive of the Father - Son and Holy Ghost -- So be it that ye shall receive - and ye shall be given as we are given - ye shall receive thy sonship -- And now it is given unto me to say unto thee: "Well done"- and ye shall pass into the Inner Temple -- And so be it and Beleis ---

I am come that ye may be rewarded for thy faithful service and loyalty -- And so be it -- And as ye are given unto modesty - ye shall receive me in the place wherein ye are - and I shall give unto thee that which I have kept for thee -- So be it and Beleis -- I am not given unto preachment - and unto many words - So I shall come unto thee in haste and make my way out - for it is not necessary to give unto thee of my words and time -- Yet ye shall receive that which I have for thee - for it shall be a token of my love and of my appreciation -- And so be it ye shall receive that which has been promised unto thee -- And so be it and Beleis ---

Now may I say that there are none which have set themself up so wise that they know what goes on behind the scene! - for they have drawn their blinds - and they see not - for it is given unto them to think themself wise! - and there are none so foolish -- So be it that they shall be reminded of their foolishness - and they shall be as ones shorn of all their self-given glory - and of all their pride and of all their wanton -- And they shall humble themself and they shall be better for it -- So be it and Beleis ---

Be ye as one which knows wherein ye are staid - and wherein ye may find comfort - and ye shall be brot into the place wherein I am -- And there shall be great joy and much gladness -- So be it and Selah -- I am thy Brother and Sibor - and one which shall come unto thee in the time which is near -- So be it and Beleis -- I am Zamu - of the Inner Temple and of the Temple of Osiris - and of the Emerald Cross---

* * *

Sananda

Blest of my being: Be ye at peace and poise - and ye shall receive of the Father - Son and Holy Ghost -- So be it and Beleis -- Now ye shall receive that which I have kept for thee for this time -- For ye have asked naught for thyself - and ye have given of thyself that they may receive and so be it that ye shall now receive that which I have for thee - and it shall serve thee well - for it shall be thy passport into all the secret places wherein ye may go - and ye shall be as one free to go and come at will -- And so be it and Beleis ---

I am come that ye may receive that which shall be my reward and my token of appreciation -- And now ye shall be prepared to receive me - for I shall come unto thee and I shall bring one which ye know - and ye shall receive us into thy place of abode - and ye shall give unto the Father thanks - for ye shall be brot out of the place wherein ye are and ye shall be given that which is promised unto thee -- So be it and Beleis --

Now ye shall add this part unto our blessed Brother Zamu's - and ye shall send it unto them which are responsible for getting it into the hands of them which are to receive it -- So be it and Beleis -- I am thy Brother - thy Sibor - and thy Director - Sananda ---

Blest of my being: Be ye prepared to receive that which shall be given unto thee of the blessed One which ye know as Coro - for he has kept a part for thee - and it shall be given unto them with the others - and it shall be given in the Name of the Father - Son and Holy Ghost - - So be it and Beleis ---

Coro

Blessed Sister of the Emerald Cross: Be ye blest of My presence and of my being -- I am come that ye may receive that which I have kept for thee - for it shall be given unto thee with the rest of thy gifts which ye shall receive - and ye shall receive them in the Name of the Father - Son and Holy Ghost -- So be it and Beleis ---

I am one which has kept thee and nourished thee that ye may reach this day -- And when it is come that ye are brot into my place I shall receive thee with great joy and gladness -- Ye have not comprehended the joy which is ours when one is brot in - so ye shall come to know -- And so be it and Beleis -- I am prepared to receive thee - and to give unto thee of my hospitality and of my love and knowledge - so be ye prepared to receive of it - and ye shall be prepared to enter into the place wherein the Father is -- And so be it and Beleis ---

Now ye shall be brot out of the place wherein ye are - and ye shall be put into a new place - and ye shall be given a new part - and ye shall receive thy inheritance in full -- So be it and Beleis -- I am come that ye may receive of the Father - Son and Holy Ghost -- So be it and Beleis

And now ye shall pass into the place of the Most High - and ye shall partake of the "Mana" and ye shall be prepared - and ye shall return into the world of men as the emissary of the Most High Living God -- So be it and Beleis -- And I am glad -- I am thy Sibor - thy Sponsor - and thy Brother of the Inner Temple and of the Brotherhood of the Emerald Cross and of the School of the Seven Rays -- So be it and Selah -- I am Coro ---

* * *

Blest of my being: Be prepared to receive of our blessed Sister of Light Nada - and that which she has for thee -- And it shall be added unto the others in the Name of the Father - Son and Holy Ghost -- So be it and Beleis ---

Nada

Blessed Sister of the Emerald Cross: Be ye blest of my being and of my presence - for I too come to add my gift unto the rest -- And ye shall be blest thereby - for I have kept mine for thee - and it shall be given unto thee in the Name of the Father - Son and Holy Ghost -- Amen and Beleis ---

Be ye as one which knows wherein ye are staid - and that which has been unto thee thy fortune which is given unto thee of them which have succored thee -- Now it is come that ye shall be brot out of the place wherein ye are - and ye shall be as one with wings upon thy feet and ye shall be given unto as we are given -- And ye shall pass into the places wherein we are with ease - and with the authority which is given unto us of the Father - and ye shall know no barriers -- And so be it and Beleis ---

I am come as my other Brothers and Sisters that ye may receive of the Father - Son and Holy Ghost - So be it that ye shall receive - and I am glad! And now ye shall go into the place of the Most High and ye shall receive thy sonship and ye shall be given thy inheritance in full - So be it and Beleis -- I am within the place wherein the Father is - and there is much cause for rejoicing -- And ye shall come to know what we mean when we say: "cause for rejoicing"- for ye of the Earth know not joy such as ours - and when one is liberated - it is great cause! For this do we work - and for this do we give thanks unto the Father -- So be it and Beleis -- I am thy Sister Nada - of the Emerald Cross ---

* * *

Blest of my being: Be ye prepared to receive of the Father - Son and Holy Ghost -- So be it and Beleis -- Be ye now prepared to receive that which is prepared for thee by our blessed Sister of Light Sarea - for she has prepared a part for them which shall be given in the Name of the Father - Son and Holy Ghost -- So be it and Beleis ---

Sarea

Beloved of my being: Be ye at peace and poise - and ye shall receive of the Father - Son and Holy Ghost -- So be it and Selah -- I am come that ye shall receive - and ye shall be brot out of darkness - and ye shall be given that which shall be given unto them which seek thee out -- So be it and Beleis -- I am one which has been upon the Altar of the Flame and I have guarded It - and I have read therein that which ye have accomplished in thy sojourn.

And I have given unto thee that which has been unto thee strength and courage - and ye have taken it and molded it into thy news form - for ye have created a new body for thyself -- And now ye shall receive it into the outer world of form - for it is given unto thee to be reborn - and ye shall be as one which steps forth into thy new body made whole for ye have gone out from the Father and Mother in parts - and now ye shall gather up thyself and return unto Them whole --

And it is fortuned unto many to be gathered in - for in the time which is near ye shall stand upon the High Holy Mount - and ye shall see that which shall occur within the Earth - and upon the Earth - and in the realm of man -- For it shall be given unto them which have been lifted up to have a part in this great plan -- And it shall be revealed in all its details unto them which are so prepared -- For it is the day of revelation - and the ones which so prepare themself shall partake of all that we have - all that we know - and all that which the Father has for them -- So be it and Selah ---

I am come that they may know these things - and that they may be prepared -- For it is given unto me to see and know that which is before them! I know the joy which is fortuned unto them which know as we know -- I know the sorrow and despair of them which are not prepared, them which are in darkness - them which do not know -- And so be it that there shall be many sent that they may know and that they may receive that which shall be their freedom -- And so be it and Selah ---

I am the keeper of the Flame and the Reader of the Records - and I have been unto my station true - and I know that of which I speak -- I come that they may share my fortune -- So be it and Selah-- I am thy Sister of the Inner Temple and of the Emerald Cross - Sarea---

Recorded by Sister Thedra

Part #54

Beloved of my being: Be ye prepared to receive that which is prepared for thee by our blessed Brother of Light - and that which he has for them -- For he has given of himself that they may receive that which he has received of the Father and of the Son and Holy Ghost -- So be it given unto them in His Name -- So be it and Beleis ---

Sornea

Beloved of the Emerald Cross: I am come unto thee from out of the Inner Temple and I am one which has held thee close and dear - and I have given of myself that ye may come to this day wherein ye may receive me - and of me -- And now that it is come ye shall be given that which we thy Sibors and Benefactors have kept for thee -- And so be it and Beleis ---

I am one which has watched thy progress - and I have given unto thee as ye have been able to receive - for have ye not been well schooled in the laws of the Losoloes? And have ye not remembered thy being within the places which are now submerged beneath the two oceans? And were ye not one of them which fled before the sinking of Posedon, were we not warned? And did we not hear and heed the warning? And did we not give credit unto them which warned us? And so was it given unto us to see Her sink into the waters wherein She remains -- And were we not sick at heart for our fellow beings which sank with Her?

And again it is given unto us to be among them which sank with the Posedon - and again it is given unto us to say unto them which we said before: "Prepare thyself!"-- And they shall hear - and they shall prepare themself -- And yet there shall be some which shall say: "Oh - it is the same ones which are crying 'disaster'!-- And they shall be unto themself traitor - for it is given into them to be beguiled by the black dragon -- And it is said: "he lies in wait"- and so truly said! For he rejoices at their sorrow -- And so be it that he shall be removed - for too long has he held sway ---

Now the "forces of light" shall be so great that he shall be consumed and he shall no longer prey upon them within the realm of man - for the Father has so willed it that all be given their freedom and for that have we revealed ourself -- So be it and Beleis -- I have spoken from out of the place wherein the Father is - and ye shall be given comprehension to understand that which I have said unto thee -- So be it and Selah -- I am thy Brother and Sibor of the Inner Temple - and of the Temple of

Tau - and of the Emerald Cross - and of Osiris -- So be it and Selah -- Sornea ---

* * *

Blest of my being: Be ye prepared to receive of that which is prepared for thee by our blessed Brother of Light - Boran - for he has a part for them which shall be given unto them in the Name of the Father Son and Holy Ghost -- So be it and Beleis ---

Boran

Blest of my being and of my presence: Be ye blest of the Father which has sent me unto thee - for that have I come that ye may be blest -- And now it is come that ye shall be brot out of the place wherein ye are and ye shall be received into the place wherein I am - and ye shall see and know that which we see and know -- And ye shall give thanks unto the Father that ye have been brot out of darkness - and for that shall ye be given thy sonship -- And so be it and Beleis --

I am given unto seeing and knowing that which shall be and that which has gone before - and it is given unto me to know that ye have been prepared for a new part -- And forget not that many have groomed thee for it -- And so be it that each has kept a gift for thee and ye shall be presented these as ye pass before each of them -- And there are great preparations within the place wherein ye shall be received - so be ye prepared - and ye shall be glad for thy preparation -- So be it and Beleis I am thy Brother and Benefactor - and Sibor - Boran.

* * *

Blest of my being: Be ye prepared to receive that which our blessed Brother of Light - Balmura has for thee - and it shall be given unto them in the Name of the Father - Son and Holy Ghost -- So be it and Beleis

Balmura

Blest of my presence and of my being: Be ye prepared - for in the time which is nigh ye shall be brot into my place and ye shall see as we see and ye shall come to know how small thy world is! - and how little ye of the Earth know - for it is given unto us to see all parts of thy Earth at one time -- And with the flip of a switch we can see thru into the core thereof -- And we can analyze all that we see within the Earth and know to the most accurate part which we are analyzing - and it is given unto us to be as thy Benefactors --

For as ye have grown to maturity we have portioned out that which ye have received - and that which ye have given thyself credit for! And did we not give unto thee the laws which govern all thy findings - and did we not direct thee into the path whereupon ye found them? And now it is come when they which have taken credit for their findings shall be brot to account - for they shall be caught up short - and they shall remember their Benefactors ---

And it is come that they which remember shall be given in abundance - and they shall be blest - for they shall be brot out of the Earth and they shall be sibored in the laws of the Losoloes and they shall return as the Sibors of the new Earth -- For it shall be given unto them of the Father - and no man shall call them a fraud - nor shall they take from them that which they have been given -- And it is given unto some to pilfer their knowledge and then credit themself for their findings -- Oh - poor in spirit are they - for they know not that the Father has endowed them with all that He has! And so be it that they shall learn the hard way -- So be it and Beleis ---

I am come that they may know that which they have inherited -- So be it and Beleis -- I am one which has watched and waited for them which are prepared to receive of the new dispensation and they shall be brot out and sibored in the laws which we are proficient in - and they shall return and give unto thee that which they have learned -- And so be it the better part of wisdom to seek them out - and ye shall be rewarded -- So be it and Beleis -- I am thy Brother and Sibor - Balmura of the Inner Temple and of the Temple of Tau - and Osiris - and of the Emerald Cross ---

* * *

Blest of my being: Be ye prepared to receive of our blessed Grand Master - for he has prepared a part for thee - and ye shall receive him in the Name of the Father - Son and Holy Ghost -- So be it and Belois

The Grand Master

Blest of my being: Be ye blest of my presence - for I am come unto thee from out of the Inner Temple wherein ye shall go and wherein ye shall receive thy Sonship -- I am one which has kept a gift for thee and ye shall receive it with the others and ye shall be glad! So be it and Selah -- In the time which is near ye shall be brot out of the Earth and ye shall be brot into the place wherein I am and ye shall be given that which we have prepared for thee - and ye shall return unto them of the world of men and ye shall give unto them as ye have received -- For it is come when we of the realms of light shall sponsor thee and we stand ready to be unto thee all that ye shall need - for thy needs shall all be filled- and ye shall be one of us -- For it is given unto us to receive of the Father - Son and Holy Ghost - So be it and Beleis ---

And now ye shall go into thy new place prepared to receive of them which shall prepare thee for the place wherein I am -- And there shall be great joy and much gladness -- So be it and Selah -- I am come that ye may receive of the Father - Son and Holy Ghost -- So be it and Beleis I am thy fortune unto the Father - and so be it and Beleis -- I am He which is known as the Grand Master of the Inner Temple ---

* * *

Blest of my being: Ye shall now receive of our blessed Brother of Light Bernard - and that which he has for them -- And so be it given in the Name of the Father - Son and Holy Ghost -- So be it and Beleis ---

Bernard - on "The Federation of Brotherhoods"

Blessed Sister of the Emerald Cross: Be ye blest of me and of the Father - Son and Holy Ghost -- So be it and Beleis ---

I am come that the veil of mystery may be removed - and that there shall be light - and that there may be comprehension of the laws which govern these things with which we are working -- And now it is given unto me to say that there are many from the higher realms which are working among them of the world of men - in the places wherein they labor for bread --

And they sit behind the desks of the offices as executives - they labor as day laborers - and ye know them not! - for they do not reveal themself unto them which are not prepared -- Yet they work in the secret places and they give of their love and of their energy that the

Father's work may be accomplished -- They give unto them which are prepared to receive in secret - and they give unto them as the Father deems wise --

For they have communication with the Father - and with each other and this is their fortune - given unto the initiate of the Father -- And now ye shall come to know some of them - for to some it is given to go out into the world of men for that purpose -- And ye shall be prepared to receive them - for they shall seek thee out and give unto thee of their love and wisdom -- So be it the better part of wisdom that ye be prepared to receive them -- So be it and Beleis ---

I am one which has worked for the day when we may make ourself known unto thee -- And now we find many prepared to receive us and of us -- And now I shall be one of them which shall reveal myself - for I have gone the long way to bring this about -- And now I say unto thee which are so prepared - that ye shall be gathered together and ye shall be given instructions which have hitherto been kept secret for them of the very highest order of these brotherhoods --

Now it is come that many from the Inner Temple and from the Temple of Tau and Osiris are among us - and they have decreed that there shall be a "Federation of Brotherhoods"- and all which are so prepared may be brot in immediately - and prepared for the higher learning and for the Losolo -- So be it that I shall be glad to receive thee into my place wherein I am and wherein ye may be schooled in the laws which govern thy world and its inhabitants -- And they which are sent unto us to establish the Federation shall sibor thee in the Losoloes ---

And so be it that many are prepared for the first place - yet many shall learn and profit - for it is given unto us to be of the new dispensation and we shall work that ye may be prepared for the Losolo And so be it and Beleis -- Our Grand Master has given us His word that we shall not fail!- and our blessed Lord and Master - our Director Sananda - sits among us and with Him we are not alone --

And we cannot fail - for He has returned unto us that this day may come into fruit-- And it shall bear fruit of a new kind -- And ye shall be gathered up - and ye shall know Him as we know Him - we which are privileged to sit with Him in the secret places - and the secret places shall be opened up unto them so prepared -- So be it and Beleis ---

I am thy Brother one which ye shall come to know -- I am within one of the secret places within North America - and I hold an office within one of thy places of learning -- And I have given of myself that ye may have a greater part! - and I have been prepared to prepare thee So be it and Beleis -- I am thy Brother Bernard - of the Federation of Brotherhoods -- So be it and Selah --- (The Losolo is the place where the Losoloes are taught - or revealed - Sister Thedra)

* * *

Blest of my being: Be ye prepared to receive that which shall be given for them by our blessed Brother of Light - Zamu - and that which he has prepared shall be given unto them in the Name of the Father - Son and Holy Ghost -- So be it and Beleis ---

Zamu

Blest of my presence and of my being: I am come at this time that they may have more light from this realm - for I am one which has been sent into the world of men that they may be brot out of darkness and that they may comprehend the laws with which we work -- We of the higher realms of learning are always and eternally aware of our Source and from whence we came –

And we are not given unto hatred! nor are we given unto groveling in the swine's burrow! - We know wherein we are staid -- We know from whence our blessings come - and we are glad for our knowing -- And we give credit where credit is due - we know our Benefactors for what they are - and we give thanks for them and for that which they give unto us - we give unto them credit for that which they give unto us --

And they are but the handmaidens of the Father - and they have prepared a table before us - and we have but to reach out in the Name of the Father - Son and Holy Ghost - and receive it -- And such is the fortune of them which are mindful of their being - and so be it that many shall be given comprehension of the fullness of their inheritance. And so be it and Beleis -- I am one which has received my inheritance in full - and I know the fullness of the Father's bounty --

So be it that ye too shall come to know - and for that have we worked without ceasing - and now ye shall be given in greater measure for it is come that all may receive of His fullness - and ye shall be brot out of darkness - and ye shall know that which is given unto thee as thy inheritance -- So be it and Beleis -- I am thy Sibor Zamu - of the Federation of Brotherhoods - and of the place wherein ye which are prepared may go -- So be it and Selah ---

Recorded by Sister Thedra

Part #55

Blest of my being: Ye shall now receive that which shall be given unto them by our blessed Brother of Light - Simmeon - which has prepared a part for them - and which has gone the long way to bless them -- So be it given in the Name of the Father - Son and Holy Ghost So be it and Beleis ---

Simmeon

Blessed Sister of the Emerald Cross: Be ye blest of my being - and of my presence - for I am come that ye may be blest - and that they which receive these words may be blest -- And so be it and Beleis

Beloved ones which are yet in the world of men: - and I say the "world of men" advisedly - for they have made for themself a world separate and apart from that of the Father - and that which He has fortuned unto them -- They have created that which torments them - that which has not satisfied their longing - and that which has purchased them -- They have pursued their own will - and they have given unto themself credit for "their progress" -- And they have forgotten from whence they came - and they know not whither they goest ---

And so be it that they shall be fortuned that which they have willed unto themself - and they know not that which they have inherited of the Father -- So be it that they shall become aware of that which is given unto them of the Father - for He has willed it so ---

Now I say unto thee: That ye shall be unto them that which the Father would have thee be - for He has so willed it that ye shall be given thy sonship - and ye shall be brot out of the place wherein ye are - and ye shall go into another place wherein ye shall be prepared for the Inner Temple -- And ye shall receive therein thy new body - and thy new name -- And ye shall return unto them as the one which shall be unto them the hands of the Father and Mother made manifest --

For ye shall be given the power and authority which shall be unto them all things -- Ye shall touch them and they shall be quickened - and they shall be made whole - and ye shall give unto them as ye have received -- So be it and Beleis ---

I am one which has come unto thee within the "world of men" before ye were called from among them -- And ye received of me that which I had for thee - and that which so prepared thee that ye now receive of me and that which shall be given unto them -- And they which receive of these words shall receive me - for the word is but the beginning - "And in the beginning was the word - and the word was God"--

And so it is - and so be it that them which receive the word shall receive me -- For I have spoken that they may hear - and will it not be given unto them to hear - and to comprehend that which they hear? So be it and Beleis ---

I am thy Brother Simmeon - of the Emerald Cross - and of the Brotherhood of The Seven Rays -- So be it and Beleis ---

Blest of my being: Be ye prepared to receive that which is given unto thee of our blessed Sister of Light - Saboni - for she has a part for thee - and it shall be given unto them -- For it is come that they shall receive that which has been kept for them - for they shall know that which has been given unto them of the Father - Son and Holy Ghost --

And they shall see that which they have fortuned unto themself is but the poor part -- And they shall be made to comprehend that which is said unto them - for it is come that they shall be made to see - and to hear -- And they shall have direct communication with the Father - and they shall have no "false gods" - for they shall be given of Him - and by Him - and they shall bow down unto no false god! So be it and Beleis

Saboni

Blest of my being and of my presence - my Sister of the Emerald Cross: Be ye as my hands made manifest unto them - for I am come from out of the Inner Temple that they may know the truth - and that they may be free - and that they may know as we of the Inner Temple know -- And the Father has so willed it that they shall know and that they shall be free --

And now it is given unto me to say that ye shall be as one which shall be sent out from the inner place wherein I am - and ye shall be unto them that which shall free them -- For it shall be given unto thee to receive thy sonship even as we of the Inner Temple -- And ye shall have the authority of the Father - which has so willed unto themes which has received their sonship -- And ye shall pass among them and ye shall be unto them all that the Father would have thee be - for He has decreed that ye shall be His hands made manifest unto them -- And so be it and Beleis ---

I am one which has served to the best of my ability within the land of Italy - and wherein I gave the vows to serve the Father which had sent be out from Him -- And for my efforts was I martyred - and now it is given unto me to have a new body and a new name -- And I am free even as the Father is free - for I have returned unto Him as one made whole - and I am free to go and to come into the Earth - and I shall --

For it is come when I shall walk among them and I shall sent them out which are prepared to receive me - for it is the day of thy new dispensation and they shall become aware of us - and they shall clean their altars - and they shall be as ones brot out of darkness -- So be it and Selah -- I am thy Sister Saboni - of the Inner Temple and of the Emerald Cross -- So be it and Selah ---

* * *

Blest of my being: Be ye prepared to receive of our blessed Brother of Light - Sornica - and that which he has prepared for them - and it shall be given unto them in the Name of the Father - Son and Holy Ghost -- So be it and Beleis ---

Sornica Secorum

Blest of my being: Be ye blest of my presence and of my being - for I am come unto thee from out of the place wherein ye shall be prepared for the Inner Temple -- And ye shall be brot into this place for thy preparation and ye shall see what goes on within this place - for there are many within this place which have received their sonship -- And they are equal unto the Father - for it is given unto them to be one with Him - and He has willed unto them His estate -- And they have free concourse into the place wherein He is - And He has given unto them power and authority to bring thee into the place wherein He is -- So be it and Selah ---

And now I say unto them which have no knowledge of the working of a brotherhood such as ours - that there shall be many strange things occur which ye may not comprehend - yet ye shall be given comprehension if ye but will it -- And ye have but to call out in the Name of the Father - Son and Holy Ghost and ye shall be answered -- For it is given unto us to be the handmaidens of the Father - and as ye call unto Him He sends us unto thee that ye may be enlightened of Him thru us -- So be it and Selah ---

I am one which has given of myself that ye may be enlightened -- And so shall ye come to know that there are many which stand ready to serve thee in the light of the Christ - which we represent unto thee - And ye shall be brot out of darkness - and ye shall see the light of the Christ - and walk therein -- So be it and Selah ---

I am one which sits in council with our blessed Lord and Master Sananda - and He has given His word that there shall be a great awakening - and a great gathering in - and He is not to be reckoned with for as He has decreed - so be it -- And as He is given unto finishing that which He begins - I know that He shall be rewarded for His labors. And so be it and Beleis ---

I say unto thee that ye have received much which should serve to awaken thee - and yet I see thee in thy lethargy sorely oppressed and sorely put out - for ye have given unto thyself the husks from the belly of the swine - when all that the Father has is thine -- So be ye as one which knows wherein ye are staid and arise and dust thyself and be as on which can find thy way - for it has been said: "Ye have the key in thy hand - and ye have but to turn it" and blest shall ye be -

I am thy Brother - Sornica Secorum - of the secret place wherein ye may be prepared for the Inner Temple -- So be it and Beleis ---

* * *

Blest of my being: Be ye prepared to receive that which shall be given unto thee by our blessed Brother Bor - for he has prepared a part for thee and ye shall give it unto them which await it -- So be it and Beleis.-

Brother Bor

Be ye blest of me - and of my presence: For I come at this time that ye may have more light from this realm - and so be it that it shall profit thee -- So be it and Selah -- I am within the place wherein the Father is and wherein they have received their sonship -- And was it not given unto all to be sent out from the Father - and shall they not return unto Him? And for that have we of the Inner Temple made ourself known unto thee that ye may come to know from whence ye come and whither thou goest -- So be it that ye may be acceptable unto the "new energy" which shall be directed unto the Earth from the realms of light -- And they which are not shall find themself in the straits of darkness So be it and Beleis ---

I am prepared to be unto thee Sibor and servant - and ye have but to present thyself for preparation - and apply thyself -- So be it that many stand ready to sibor thee - and ye shall find that it shall profit thee to seek them out -- And so shall they find thee and be unto thee that which ye shall need - that which shall deliver thee-- For the time is nigh when ye shall remember my words! and ye shall call - and ye shall call again and again - and ye may be as one which has thrown overboard thy life belt! ---

So be ye as wise as a serpent (an initiate) and silent as a sphinx - and give unto the Father thy whole heart - thy will and thy energy - and ye shall be given that which shall deliver thee from bondage and darkness -- So be it and Beleis -- I am thy Guardian and Benefactor - Brother Bor - of the Inner Temple -- So be it and Selah---

* * *

Blest of my being: Be ye prepared to receive that which is prepared for thee by our blessed Sister of Light - Mura - for she has prepared a part for thee - and it shall be given unto them which are prepared to receive it - in the Name of the Father - Son and Holy Ghost -- So be it and Beleis ---

Mura

Blest of my being - my Sister of the Emerald Cross - and be ye blest of my presence -- And now it is come that ye shall be brot into the place wherein I am - and ye shall receive thy sonship - and ye shall be prepared to return unto them of the world of men -- Ye shall be given thy new part within the time which is near -- And ye shall be as we are. ye shall be free to go and come into the place wherein we are - and into the Earth at will - and no man shall stay thee nor shall he be unto thee a bond ---

For it shall not be given unto man to have the power to say where - or when ye shall go -- And he shall stand in awe of thy power and of thy authority -- Yet it is given unto every one to be the sons of God - and they have but to claim their sonship -- And so be it and Selah -- I am come that they may know that which is their heritage -- It is given unto me to command the "Crystal Bell Fleet" which are part of a guardian fleet which has been drawing nearer and nearer unto the Earth -- And it is given unto us to be the fortune of the planet Venus and as ye have been told - "there are many which stand guard" - yet they have not come in so close unto thy horizon - and few have come even into thy world - yet the fleet remained past the horizon --

Now it is given unto me to be the twin flame of the blessed Brother Balmura - and as we were sent out from the Father and Mother as "one" we have remained as "one" (yet we are two) and we have not separated ourself -- For it is given unto us to work within the Father and we are one with Him - and for this do we remain united - and for that are we whole -- For it is given unto the children of the Earth to go out in parts and ye shall be brot back as one with the Father and mother and be made whole --

And they shall be united with the same flame as which he went out from the Father and Mother -- For it is given unto them which are brot back to be made whole ere they are brot into the Inner Temple - and for that have ye of the outer temples waited -- For it is given unto some to be within the realms of darkness while the part which has remained with the Father waits thy return -- So be it that there shall be a great gathering in - and many shall be united as the brides and bridegrooms of the Father --

And so be it and Selah -- I am one which shall receive thee into the Crystal Bell Fleet and I shall be unto thee thy hands and thy feet - and I shall be unto thee hostess wherein ye shall go -- So be ye prepared to enter into the Crystal Bell Fleet -- So be it and Selah -- I am thy Sister of the Inner Temple - the Temple of Osiris - and the Emerald Cross -- I am Mura ---

Recorded by Sister Thedra

Part #56

Beloved of my being: Be ye as one which has my hand upon thee and ye shall receive as I have received -- So be it and Selah -- I am come unto thee that ye may receive them which shall come unto thee -- So be it and Selah -- Now ye shall give unto them this word and it shall go out immediately -- So be it and Selah -- Sananda ---

The Father and Mother

Blessed children which I hold dear and so near: Know ye not that I am with thee? - and I am given unto waiting - for long have I awaited thy return -- So be it that the time is come when ye shall be gathered in as grain from the field -- For it is now come when ye shall remember Me and the part which ye had with Me before ye went into darkness -- So be it that ye shall have thy memory restored unto thee and ye shall be glad - and ye shall go into darkness no more - so be it ---

And for that are ye now being prepared - for it is thy heritage that ye shall return unto Me and be made perfect -- So be it and Selah I am one which has given unto thee thy "Being" and ye shall come to know Me as ye knew Me before thy going into darkness wherein thy memory has been blanked from thee -- So shall ye now receive thy inheritance in full - for ye have given unto Me thy Father credit for thy being and for that which ye shall become ---

Now it is given unto Me to receive thee as ye were before ye separated thyself from Me -- And for this have I sent my emissaries into the Earth that ye may be as ones prepared to return unto Me -- So be it that ye shall receive them in My Name and for thy sake -- And ye shall be as ones reborn and ye shall walk with the "new body" which shall be <u>created</u> <u>new</u> and which shall be like unto Myself - for I have endowed thee with that which I shall give unto thee as thy inheritance

So be it that ye shall return into darkness no more -- And for this have I sent many into the Earth that She may come into Her fullness and into Her maturity as I have so ordained -- So be it and Selah Now ye shall give unto Me <u>credit</u> <u>for</u> <u>thy</u> <u>being</u> and unto My emissaries credit for thy <u>well</u> <u>being</u> --

And ye shall come to know the law of thy "Being" and thy oneness with all things -- So be it and Selah -- I Am thy Father and thy Mother and I have given unto thee of Myself that ye may be like unto Me - and that ye may become as gods and as co-creators with Me - and ye shall have no bondage for ye shall be free and ye shall go and come at will into My place of abode - and ye shall give unto Me credit for all that which ye shall become --

For I have created thee perfect and in My image and ye shall be like unto Me - and ye shall know from whence ye have gone out - and ye shall return unto Me and be made whole -- And for this have they been sent out from My place of abode - and they shall walk among thee and they shall give unto thee as they have received of Me - for I have endowed them with My power and My Love and Wisdom and it is given unto them to know as I know and to be My hands and My feet made manifest upon the Earth -- So be it and Selah---

And they are free from the gravitation of the Earth and the attraction of the moon - and they have free concourse into My place of abode - so shall they go and come at will -- So be it and Selah -- I have given unto thee a new dispensation and ye shall be given all the plan - the fullness of this plan which is designed for thy return unto Me -- And ye shall be given comprehension that ye may find thy way --

Yet as I have said unto thee that many are sent unto thee - ye shall seek them out and ye shall follow in their footsteps - for they have prepared the way before thee - and they know the way -- They too know the law of thy "Being" - and they shall lead thee as a little child - for it is as a <u>little</u> <u>child</u> that ye shall ask of them - and they shall give unto thee as they have received of Me - So be it and Selah ---

I am come unto thee that ye may be quickened and that ye may be alert - and that ye may be prepared to receive them which I shall send unto thee -- So be it and Selah -- I Am thy Father and thy Mother - so be it that ye shall return unto Me -- Selah ---

Sananda

Beloved of my being: Be ye as my hands made manifest unto them which are to receive of me and by me --So shall ye be blest as I have been blest of the Father -- So be it and Selah -- Now ye shall give unto them my words which ye shall record and send immediately unto them.

For among them which shall receive them are some which shall be brot into my place of abode and they shall receive as I have received and they shall be as ones which shall pass the great barrier without tasting death - they shall be illumined and given new bodies - and they shall be free from the gravitation of the Earth and free from the attraction of the moon - and they shall have free concourse into any place within the galaxy and they shall have no bondage - for they shall be free even as I am free ---

For that have I returned into the Earth - that they may know that which is their inheritance willed unto them of the Father -- So be it that I shall reveal myself unto them which are prepared to receive me -- So be it and Selah ---

Now I say unto them: Beloved which are my sheep: I shall give unto thee as I have received of my Father Which has given unto me His plan for thy deliverance from bondage -- And ye shall partake of the manna for it is now come when ye have reached the age of accountability and ye shall receive that which has been held in trust for thee for this age -- So be it and Selah --

Now ye shall apply thyself diligently to thy preparation and ye shall seek out them which I shall send unto thee as my "lamp bearers" - for they shall go out before me and they shall give unto thee as they have received of me -- For as I have received my inheritance of the Father have I given unto my lamp bearers -- So be it that they shall come unto thee and they shall prepare thee as I have prepared them -- So be it and Selah ---

Now ye shall give unto the Father credit for thy "Being" and unto thy Benefactors credit for thy "well-being"-- So be it that they shall remember thee and they shall seek thee out and ye shall be glad for thy preparation -- So be it and Selah -- Now I say unto thee - that in the time which is near one shall be sent out from my place of abode and they shall come unto thee and they shall give unto thee as they have received of me -- And ye shall be glad for that which ye shall receive - for it shall renew thee and ye shall stand free as one reborn -- So be it and Selah --

It is now the <u>New</u> <u>Age</u> and ye have not yet seen or heard that which is in store for thee - so be ye as one which can comprehend that which I say unto thee and great shall be thy revelation -- So be it and Selah -- I am one which has gone before thee and I have prepared the way - and ye shall be glad for thy inheritance - which ye have but to claim in the Name of the Father - Son and Holy Ghost -- So be it and Selah -- I am thy Sibor and the Director of the New Dispensation - Sananda ---

* * *

Sananda:

Beloved: Now ye shall give unto them this word which shall be given unto thee by the blessed Brother of Light - Maheru - and ye shall give it unto them as follows:

Maheru

Beloved of my being: Be ye blest for my presence - and be ye as one which has my hand upon thee and ye shall receive as I have received. So be it and Selah -- Now ye shall record my words unto them which are to receive of their inheritance - for none other shall accept them -- So be it and Selah ---

Now I say unto them: Beloved ones which have asked for more light and which are seeking thy salvation in and thru the Father: Be ye as ones which have my hand upon thee and ye shall receive as I have received -- So be it in the Name of the lost High Living God -- I am privileged to come unto thee at this time that ye may be prepared to receive that which is every man's inheritance -- Yet some shall wait - for it is given unto them to be beguiled by the forces of darkness -- Yet they - the forces of darkness - shall be dispelled forever and man shall stand free in the Light of the Christ - and he shall know himself to be the son of God The Father -- So be it and Selah ----

So shall it behoove thee to seek the Light of the Christ while it is yet time - for I say unto thee that the time is nigh upon thee when ye shall cry out as one in despair - for it is now come when ye shall be in the straits of darkness - for the Sun shall give forth no comfort - no light for it shall be as a "bowl of blood" and it shall - find a new berth and it shall be unto another solar system the light - it is now unto the Earth.

And the Earth shall slip upon Her axis and move out into another berth as a ship at sea - for it is give unto the planet ye call Earth to be prepared for a new place - and She shall become as a sun to lesser planets yet uninhabited ---

So be it that ye shall be removed for a time into another place of habitation and for that are ye being prepared -- I am one which has given of myself that ye may be prepared -- So be it and Selah -- Now I say unto thee that the day is not afar off when ye shall be caused to remember my words - for it is given unto me to know whereof I speak.

For I have received my inheritance in full and I and the Father are one - and as I have received my inheritance I know as He knows -- And I am one which has gone the "Royal Road" and I know that which is given unto the Father to know -- For He has endowed me with all that He is and all that He has and He has given unto me of Himself - and as He is so am I -- So be it that ye too shall come into the fullness of thy being and ye shall be glad -- So be it and Selah ---

Now ye shall go out from thy present place of abode as one prepared - for ye have given unto thyself that which ye shall receive -

and ye shall be put into the place for which ye are prepared -- So it is my part to prepare thee for a place wherein is <u>light</u> - for it shall be given unto them which serve the forces of darkness to be put into a place wherein they have no light - and they shall have no science nor shall they have any memory of that which they have learned --

So be it that it is the better part of wisdom to seek the light and to be prepared for a place wherein there is light -- I say unto thee that sad indeed are the ones in darkness! Be ye as one which can comprehend that which I say unto thee - and as ye seek more comprehension more shall be revealed unto thee -- So be it and Selah -- I am thy Sibor and thy Brother - Maheru ---

Footnote: Maheru (Muru) is the former Abbott of the School of the Seven Rays (of the Brotherhood of the Seven Rays) which has its focal point on Earth at Lake Titicaca -- He has recently made his ascension - or gone the "Royal Road" - Thedra ---

* * *

Bor speaking:

Beloved of my being: Ye shall now receive that which shall be given unto thee by our beloved Brother of Light - Moraya - for he has prepared a part for them which shall go unto them immediately - and it shall be given consideration - and it shall be as the next portion. For it is now come when many shall receive of him and by him -- So be it that it be expedient that this be sent unto them immediately -- So be it and Selah -- Now ye shall receive that which he has prepared for them. So be it and Selah -- I am thy Sibor and Brother - Bor ---

Moraya

Beloved of my being: I am thy Sibor and thy older Brother – Moraya. And I have prepared thee that ye may receive of me and by me - and ye shall go into all the lands of the Earth as my emissary - for it is given unto me to give unto thee as I have received of the Father - and ye shall not weary nor shall ye want - for I shall be unto thee all that ye shall need -- So be it and Selah -- Now it is come when ye shall return unto them within thy native land and ye shall give unto them as ye have received -- So be it and Selah ---

I am come unto thee that ye may be prepared to return unto them - and it is the better part of wisdom - for it is now come when they shall be gathered together and they shall be counted one by one and none shall be missing -- So be it and Selah -- Now ye shall give unto them that which I shall give unto thee for them - and it shall be as follows:

Beloved ones which have begun to stir within thy slumbers: Be ye as ones which have my hand upon thee and I shall bless thee as I have been blest of the Father -- So shall ye be glad - for it is now come when they of other realms shall walk among thee and ye shall partake of their love and wisdom -- And ye shall be indeed wise to seek them out for they shall give unto thee that which they have received of the Father - that which is given unto them for thee -- For it is now come when ye shall be brot out of the places of darkness - and wherein is the black dragon -- For ye have been bound within these places for long - and ye have but to seek deliverance and many shall be sent out of the realms of light that ye may come into the fullness of thy inheritance ---

Before thee is a plan which has been designed to free thee from bondage forever -- Yet ye shall prepare thyself to receive of this plan - for none shall partake of this knowledge which are not prepared -- And for that do I now reveal myself that ye may come to know that which has been prepared for thee -- So be it that I shall come into the "world of men" as one made manifest within the flesh - and I shall pass among thee and I shall seek out them which are prepared to receive as I have received of the Father ---

For it is now come when many from out of the realms of light shall come into the "world of men" that the Father may be glorified within the Earth -- Now ye shall call unto the Father - the Cause of thy being, and ye shall give unto Him credit for thy being - and He shall send unto thee one which is prepared to deliver thee out of bondage -- Yet <u>ye</u> <u>shall</u> <u>will</u> <u>it</u> <u>so</u> --

And so be it and Selah -- Be ye as a little child and of the mind to accept that which is offered unto thee for it is the way which ye shall receive thy inheritance willed unto thee of the Father -- Be ye as one which can comprehend that which I say unto thee -- So be it that I shall sibor thee and as ye are prepared I shall come unto thee and I shall give unto thee as I have received - for it is now come when we of the higher realms shall walk among thee as fellow beings and as brothers - and ye shall come to know us as brothers which stand ready to give unto thee of our love and wisdom -- So shall ye be wise to prepare thyself ---

Now it is given unto me to know wherein ye are prepared -- And ye shall be unto thyself true and ye shall give unto the Father credit for thy being - and unto thy Benefactors and Sibors credit for thy well-being - for He has sent us unto thee that His will may be done in the Earth thru us -- So be it and Selah ---

Now ye shall be mindful of thy speech -- Ye shall give unto the Father praise and glory for thy being - and ye shall let no word escape from thee which is not like unto Him - for it is now come when thy words shall be made manifest before thee -- For in days past they were held in abeyance -- now they shall be loosed and ye shall see that which ye send out of thy mouth manifest before thee - for it shall be swift and sure and ye shall reap thy own reward -- And I say unto thee that bitter shall be the words upon thy tongue which are not inspired of the Christ for they shall return unto thee as fire upon thy reed ---

So be it that ye shall come to know the power of the "spoken word" and I am one which has gone the Royal Road and I know whereof I speak -- For as it was in the beginning the spoken word became manifest and there was "light"-- And it is given unto me to know for I am one with the Father and He has endowed me with the power to create in His likeness and in His image -- So be it every man's inheritance -- And for that have I come into the realm of darkness that ye may be delivered out -- So be it and Selah -- I am thy Sibor and thy Older Brother - Moraya ---

Recorded by Sister Thedra

Part #57

Beloved of my being: Be ye as one which has my hand upon thee - and ye shall receive of me as I have received of the Father -- So be it and Selah -- Now ye shall give unto them which shall be given unto thee by our blessed Brother of Light - Berean - so shall it profit them -- So be it and Selah -- I am thy Brother and thy Sibor - Sananda ---

Berean

Beloved ones which I have watched and guarded - which I have held so dear: Be ye as ones which can comprehend that which I say unto thee - for it is now come when ye shall be given great comprehension - and great shall be thy revelation - for ye have gone into darkness for the last time ---

And now ye shall be brot out of darkness without going thru the throes of rebirth - that is - thru the portals of flesh again -- For it is now come when ye shall create anew the vehicles (bodies) which ye now have -- They shall be illumined and ye shall step from the port of darkness into the one of light - and it shall serve thee -- And ye shall no longer be its servant - for ye shall have perfect control and command over that which ye shall call thy body -- And ye shall be free to leave it at will - for it shall not bind thee -- And ye shall create perfectly as the Father has so willed - so be it thy inheritance---

And now I say unto thee for the first time that ye shall be as one resurrected from the dead - for ye are the "living dead" - ye know not freedom! nor do ye know the meaning of thy being - for ye have forgotten thy Source -- Now it shall be given unto thee to remember - and for that do I now reveal myself -- For now in the age which is come, the age of the new dispensation - ye shall have thy memory restored and ye shall know the Source of thy being - and ye shall be co-creators with the Father and ye shall be free to go and to come into His place of abode ---

For this have many been sent unto thee - so be it that ye shall come to know them as fellow beings - for the mystery shall be removed forever! So be it and Selah -- I am one which shall give unto thee as I have received of the Father - for He has given unto me the power and the wisdom which He has willed unto me that I may come unto thee at this time -- And I shall sibor thee as ye are prepared to receive-- Now ye shall be given all the truth - and not in part -- Yet ye shall be prepared to receive it - for it is not given unto thee more than ye can consume -- Forget not that the babe at the breast is not given the flesh of animals - and yet ye shall grow in strength and understanding -- So be it and Selah.

I am one which has brot ye into this age wherein we thy Sibors may make ourselves known unto thee and wherein we may bring thee out of thy own self-created hell -- So be it and Selah -- I am now come unto thee at this time that ye may have more light -- So be it that many have come - and ye shall be wise to seek them out - for they shall come unto thee and sibor thee - and ye shall know them -- So be it the better part of wisdom that ye be prepared to receive them -- So be it and Selah ---

Now it is come when they shall walk among thee and they shall not reveal themselves until ye are prepared to receive them -- So shall it behoove thee to prepare thyself to receive that which they are prepared to give unto thee -- So be it and Selah -- I am come unto thee that ye may be brot out of darkness and that ye may receive the "greater part"- So be it and Selah -- Be ye as one which has my hand upon thee and I shall give unto thee as I have received - for I have received my inheritance in full - so shall ye come to know the fullness of thy inheritance -- For ye shall go out from wherein ye are into another which has been prepared for thee and ye shall be as one prepared for the place wherein ye shall go -- For it is given unto thee to have a new place of abode - as shall the Earth --- For it is now come when all the planets are moving into new ports - and wherein there shall be much greater light ---

Ye shall be given more on that subject by others - for it is my part to prepare a place wherein ye may go in "peace and harmony" and wherein ye shall know no sorrow -- For many shall have much sorrow and suffering - yet it need not be - for many have been sent from out of the realms of light that they may be delivered out before the day of sorrow -- And now ye shall give unto them ear - for they have given of themselves that ye may know thy freedom -- So be it that ye shall be wise to hear that which they say unto thee -- So be it and Selah -- I am thy Sibor and thy Benefactor - Berean ---

Footnote: Berean is one of the Eloheim and one of the twenty four Elders - - Sister Thedra ---

* * *

Beloved of my being: Now ye shall receive that which shall be given unto them by our blessed Brother of Light - Soreto -- So be it and Selah. I am thy Sibor - Sananda ---

Soreto

Beloved ones which are yet in the "world of men": Be ye as ones which shall be brot out - for that have I now revealed myself unto thee -- For I have come unto thee with the Divine consent of our Father - and He has decreed that ye shall come into the place wherein He is and ye shall be as one prepared -- For that has the key unto thy legirons been given unto thee -- Yet it shall be kept ever before thee that ye may not say ye knew not: "Father - Thy Will be done in me - thru me - by me - and for me"- it shall be thy passport into His of abode - for He shall not deny thee when ye come unto Him in the manner ---

So be it that the day of the new dispensation is come when He has given unto thee a safer and quicker passage -- For it is now come when many from out of the realms of light have come into the Earth that ye may be brot out immediately -- And ye need no longer have the part of rebirth and death unto the physical body - for ye shall master that which is thy physical body and ye shall control the elements and triumph over death --

And for that do many reach out unto thee that ye may become <u>master</u> <u>of</u> <u>all</u> <u>things</u> in love - wisdom and prudence -- So be it and Selah. I am one which has given of myself that these things may be as part of thee - for it is willed unto thee of the Father - and ye shall receive as ye are prepared to receive -- And for that have many come unto the Earth that ye too may be lifted up -- So be it and Selah ---

Now ye shall come to know that which I have said unto thee - for it is the day of revelation when ye shall stand free of all thy bonds - all thy bondage - and ye shall be as one who knows and knows that he knows -- Ye shall no longer be bound by the opinions of others for ye shall know as the Father knows - and ye shall walk in the Light of the Christ forever -- So be it and Selah -- I am thy Sibor and thy Older Brother - Soreto -- (One of the 24 Elders and one of the Guardians of the Earth since Her beginning - Sister Thedra) ---

Beloved of my being: Ye shall now record for them that which shall be given unto them from our Brother of Light - Sorica -- So be it and Selah -- I am thy Director and thy Sibor - Sananda ---

Sorica

Beloved child of Earth - which I have watched and guarded: Be ye as one which has my hand upon thee and I shall bless thee as I have been blest of the Father -- So be it and Selah -- I am come unto thee that they may be given that which I have prepared for them - so be it ye shall be blest and ye shall know no sorrow -- So be it and Selah -- I am thy Sibor and I have so prepared thee that ye may receive of me and by me -- So be it and Selah -- Now ye shall say unto them that which I shall give unto thee for them - and it shall serve to awaken them from their lethargy -- So be it and Selah ---

Beloved children - which have begun to stir in thy slumber: Will ye not arouse thyself - alert thyself and hear that which we thy Sibors are saying unto thee? Have ye not been given much? Yet ye sink again and again into lethargy -- Now it is come when ye shall be given a portion which shall bring thee out of thy lethargy - and it shall serve to keep thee alert and awake - for it is the better part of wisdom that ye stay awake --

So be it and Selah -- Now ye shall be prepared to receive this portion - for none other shall receive it -- And for this are many sent out from the place wherein I am and they but await thy preparation - for they are alert and they know wherein ye are and they are at the Father's business and know as He knows ---

And He has given into them the power and wisdom to deliver thee out of thy bondage -- Now ye shall say: What is this ye are saying unto me? And I shall say unto thee that which has been said many times before - "That it is the day of the new dispensation - the New Order - when each and every one shall be removed from the Earth into a new place of abode"--

And there are many places and each different from the other - yet ye the children of the Earth are different - and as ye are prepared so the place is prepared - for it is given unto thee according to thy preparation and is it not the law? For it is so ordered that the Earth shall pass out of her present place wherein She is into one wherein is more light - and She shall be groomed for Her new part ---

And ye have had much on that - and ye shall have more! For it is given unto me to know them which are prepared to read the records wherein all things are recorded - and ye shall be given as ye are prepared to receive -- So be it and Selah -- Blest are they which are prepared - for great shall be thy revelation! Now ye shall give me credit for preparing thee - for I know the sorrow of them which shall be found unprepared -- So be it and Selah --

Now ye have given unto others credit for thy well-being and for thy sorrow - yet I say unto thee: ye have fortuned unto thyself all thy sorrow all thy torment -- So be it that ye shall come to know the law which ,governs thy being - and ye shall come to know the ones which have guarded thee and kept thee - and ye shall give unto them credit for thy well-being and ye shall learn to say: "Father - Thy Will be done in me thru me - by me - and for me"-- And ye shall surrender thy will - and thy heart as thy "living sacrifice" unto Him - for thy prayer of hollow words which are as but rigamaroles shall avail thee naught -- So be it that ye bring unto Him thyself and thy whole being - as He has endowed thee with all that ye are - all that ye have - and all that ye shall become! So shall it behoove thee to make haste - for many have gone before thee and they have prepared the way -- And ye shall follow in their footsteps. So be it and Selah -- I am thy older Brother and thy Benefactor - Sorica-

Sananda

Beloved of my being: Be ye as one which has my hand upon thee and I shall bless thee as I have been blest -- So be it and Selah -- I am thy Sibor and I have so prepared thee that ye may receive as I have received. so be it in the Name of the most High Living God -- So be it and Selah -- Now ye shall give unto them these words which shall serve them well -- So be it and Selah -- I am come unto thee that they may receive that which I shall say unto them --

So be it that ye shall be blest of me as I have been blest - and ye shall know no sorrow -- So be it and Selah -- I am thy Sibor and I have so prepared thee that ye may receive them which are sent out from the realms of light - and I have stood porter at the gate that none from the realms of darkness may pass -- So be it that this port shall be kept pure that ye may receive of the Father - Son and Holy Ghost -- So be it and Selah -- I am thy Sibor and the Director of the New Dispensation -- So be ye as one which has my hand upon thee and ye shall receive as I have received -- So be it and Selah -- I am Sananda ---

Beloved ones which I call my own: Have ye not heard that which has been said unto thee - and are ye not mindful of all the preparations which are being made on thy behalf and for thy deliverance? Now it is come when ye shall be given much which shall serve to awaken thee - and ye shall be quickened - for it is now the age of light when the Earth and Her children are going thru great initiations which shall prepare them for a new place --

Now ye shall question many things which shall be said unto thee - yet I am one which can speak with authority - for I have read the records and I know the law - for the Father has given unto me my inheritance and I know as He knows -- So be it and Selah -- Now it is come when ye shall receive of me as I have received of Him - so shall ye come to know the law of oneness of thy being -- So be it and Selah -- I am thy Sibor and thy Brother - Sananda ----

* * *

Beloved of my being: Now ye shall give unto them this portion - for it has been kept for this time and it shall serve them well -- So be it and Selah -- Sananda ---

Mother Sara

Beloved ones which I have held so close and so dear: Will ye not hear that which I say unto thee? For it is given unto Me to be thy Mother - thy fortune unto the Father -- So be it that ye shall come to know Me - for I shall go into the "world of men" in the garment of flesh that ye may know Me and that ye may receive of Me and by Me -- For ye have been in the world of darkness for long and ye have forgotten Me and the part which ye had with Me -- Now it is come when ye shall remember and ye shall return unto Me and ye shall come into My place of abode as one prepared - and ye shall be glad for thy preparation -- So be it and Selah ---

Now ye shall be as ones which have been asleep and which have awakened from a long sleep which has been troubled and tormented - and ye shall be glad ye have awakened -- So be it and Selah -- Will ye not receive that which I shall bring unto thee? for it shall free thee forever - and ye shall be as one delivered out of bondage - out of hell - for it is the part which ye have created for thyself and now ye are offered thy freedom --

For that shall I come unto thee in the world made flesh -- So be it that ye shall ask to receive Me and as ye are prepared I shall come unto thee and I shall give unto thee that which I have kept for thee and ye shall rejoice forevermore -- So be it and Selah -- Be ye as one which has My hand upon thee and I shall bless thee - and I shall pass among thee and I shall seek thee out as ye are prepared to receive Me -- So be it and Selah -- Be ye as one which has a mind to receive Me and of Me - for it is the law which not even I shall break -- So be it and Selah -- I am thy Mother - fortune of the Father -- So be it and Selah ---

Recorded by Sister Thedra

Part #58

Beloved of my being: Ye shall now receive for them that which shall be given unto them by the beloved Brother - Michael - for he has prepared a part for them -- So be it and Selah -- I am thy Director and Sibor - Sananda ---

Michael

Beloved which I have held so dear: Ye shall now give unto them that which I have prepared for them -- For it is now come when they shall come to know me and the part which I have prepared for them -- Be ye as my hands made manifest unto them and ye shall receive of me as I have received of the Father -- So be it and Selah ---

Beloved ones which I call my sheep: Be ye as ones which have my hand upon thee and I shall bring thee out of the place wherein ye are and ye shall be brot into a place wherein is much light and wherein ye shall know no sorrow or suffering - for I have prepared a place and now

I am ready to receive thee -- So be it and Selah -- Be ye as one which can comprehend that which we thy Sibors say unto them --

For it is now come when ye shall be given much which is designed to prepare thee - so be it that ye shall be glad for thy preparation -- Now ye shall stand still and hear me - for it is given unto me to know whereof I speak - for I am one which has guarded thee from the beginning of thy earthly habitation - and I have watched thee and I have waited for the day when I may come unto thee as I now come unto my recorder - and that I may counsel thee and be unto thee Sibor -- For great is thy inheritance - and ye have groveled within the swine's burrow for pittance.

Now it is come when ye are offered thy freedom - thy inheritance which is willed unto thee of the Father and which is in no wise a poor pittance! for He has given of Himself that ye may have thy being and all that He is He has willed unto thee -- So shall He give unto thee that which is fortuned unto thee - as ye are prepared to receive - so be it the law - "as ye are prepared ye shall receive"-- So be it and Selah ---

Be ye as one mindful of thy Source - for ye have given little thot unto the Source of thy Being - and now it is come when ye shall call unto the Father for help - for ye shall be caught up short and ye shall have need of help -- And for that has He sent me unto thee that ye may not know sorrow - for the day of much sorrow is nigh upon thee - So be it that ye shall be prepared to be brot out before - so shall it profit thee -- So be it and Selah --

I am one which has kept thee and I have given of myself that ye may be comforted -- So be it and Selah -- Now I say unto thee - be mindful of thy Source and be ye true unto thyself and seek thy salvation within the Father - and ye shall be sent one which shall give unto thee the "portion" which shall serve thee well -- So be it and Selah ---

And ye shall rejoice forevermore! So be it and Selah -- I am one which shall come into the "world of men" and I shall give unto them which are prepared to receive me as I have received of the Father -- So be it and Selah -- Now I say unto thee - be ye prepared to receive them which shall be sent into the world of men that ye may be lifted up - for He has given unto thee a new dispensation which is designed to free each and every one which shall accept of His bounty and His wisdom His love and mercy --

I ask of thee only one thing: surrender up thy whole self wholeheartedly that ye may receive as I have received - for that do I now come unto thee and ye shall be glad! So be it and Selah -- I am one which has gone the "Royal Road" and I know every step of the way and I shall be unto thee hand and foot -- So be it and Selah -- I am thy Older Brother and Sibor - known as Prince Michael - the Shepherd --- (The recorder knows him as Prince Michael - while he is also known as Archangel Michael

* * *

Beloved: ye shall now give unto them this portion which shall be given unto thee by our beloved Brother of Light - Sanat Kumara - so shall it profit them -- So be it and Selah -- I am thy Sibor and thy Brother - Sananda ---

Sanat Kumara

Beloved children of Earth: Have I not waited for this day when ye shall be brot out of darkness - and have I not given of myself that ye may have freedom? Now it is come when ye shall move into greater realms of light and ye shall know thyself to be "Sons of God" the Father -- And ye shall be as ones which have been delivered out of hell - that which ye have fortuned unto thyself --

Now it is come when ye shall walk and counsel with thy brothers of light from the realms of light wherein all things are known and wherein there is no sorrow -- And for that have many come into the Earth that ye may be lifted up -- So shall ye profit to know them and to receive of them and by them - for the day of thy deliverance is come - ye have but to receive it - to accept it -- So be it and Selah -- I am come unto thee that ye may be delivered up - for as it has been said unto thee many times - "the day of sorrow is nigh upon thee"-- Yet ye need not suffer more - for many stand ready to bring thee out before that dreadful day when the sun shall give forth no light and when the Earth shall be as one in agony --

So be it that ye shall be prepared for a new place of abode - and ye shall seek the light and it shall be revealed unto thee -- And for that have many been sent into the Earth -- Ye shall seek them out and they shall reveal themself unto thee and they shall give unto thee that which shall quicken thee and which shall be unto thee thy deliverance -- Yet it is the law that ye prepare thyself to receive their "gifts" for it is given unto them to be sent out by the Father and they come bearing gifts which are above price - more precious than gold - frankincense and myrrh - so be it that ye shall be wise to prepare thyself to receive them.

For they shall pass among thee and they shall seek out them which are prepared to receive them – So be it and Selah I have given unto thee just a small part of which I have for thee - and as ye are prepared I shall come unto thee and sibor thee and I shall give unto thee as I have received of the Father -- For it is now come when ye shall know the fullness of thy inheritance -- So be it and Selah -- I am thy Brother and thy Sibor - Sanat Kumara ---

* * *

Beloved of my being" Ye shall now receive that which shall be given unto thee by our beloved Sister of Light - Berea - So be it and Selah -- I am Sananda ---

Berea

Beloved of my being: Be ye as one which has my hand upon thee and ye shall receive of me and by me and ye shall give unto others as ye have received -- So be it and Selah -- Now ye shall be my hands made manifest unto them which are prepared to receive my words -- and I shall say unto them as I have said unto thee - they shall receive of me as I have received of the Father -- So be it and Selah ---

Beloved children of the Earth which are seeking the light wherein ye shall find thy deliverance: Be ye blest of my presence - for I now come unto thee that ye may receive as I have received of the Father -- So be it and Selah -- I am one which has stood by the Earth and Her children thru many initiations and thru many trials --

Now it is come when the Earth shall move out of Her present berth into another wherein She shall receive Her great inheritance - for She is designed to become the "garden of the solar system" -- So be it that the inhabitants of the Earth shall be removed for a period of time and they which are prepared shall partake of the Earth's inheritance - and they shall return unto Her and they shall know no sorrow -- For it is given unto Her to be purified and renewed and to become a sun unto lesser planets -- So be it part of that which shall be revealed unto thee. So be it and Selah -- I am thy Sister of Venus - Berea --

Berea is the twin flame or complement of our beloved Sanat Kumara--

* * *

Beloved of my being: Ye shall now receive that which is to be sent unto them - and it shall serve to bring them out of their lethargy -- So be it and Selah -- Sananda ---

Sananda

Beloved ones which I call my own: Is it not the better part of wisdom that ye be prepared for that which shall come upon thee and that which shall be given unto thee? So be it that there shall be a loud voice ring out and it shall be heard in all the lands of the Earth! and ye shall hear it and ye shall follow it - so be it that it shall profit thee –

So be it and Selah -- Now it is come when ye shall have great trials and tribulations - and ye shall cry: "Lord! Lord!" and ye shall be as one in the valley of despair -- So be it that it shall behoove thee to seek thy deliverance while it is yet time - and for that have many come into the Earth which are prepared to deliver thee -- And as I have said unto thee many times that ye shall seek them out and they shall come unto thee and they shall give unto thee as they have received of the Father -- So be it and Selah –

I am calling unto thee! and I am speaking unto thee! and yet ye have not given unto me credence - nor have ye heard that which I have said unto thee - for ye are drunken on the wine of thy own making and ye are as blind unto the light which we shed upon thee -- So shall ye be sobered! and ye shall be alert - and ye shall hear and see! So be it and Selah -- I am come that ye may be sobered - that ye may walk with equilibrium and that ye may see the Light of the Christ and walk in it forever -- So be it and Selah -- I am thy Sibor and the Director of the New Dispensation - Sananda ---

* * *

Beloved of my being: Be ye as one which has my hand upon thee and ye shall receive of me and by me -- So be it and Selah -- Now ye shall receive that which I have prepared for them -- So be it and Selah -- I am thy Brother Bor ---

Beloved children of Earth: Be ye blest of my presence - for I come unto thee out of the Inner Temple that ye may be blest as I have been blest -- So be it and Selah -- I am one of the Kumaras and I too have watched thy tribulations and thy sorrows -- And it is given unto me to come unto thee that ye may have no more sorrow - no more suffering. So be it that ye shall be prepared for a new place of abode and I have been in these places which are prepared and I am one which has so prepared them - I know whereof I speak -- For it is given unto me of the Father that I may come unto thee at this time that ye may have more light and that ye may be delivered out of bondage ---

So be it that ye shall come to know me as ye shall know thy other Brothers which have come unto thy rescue -- For ye know not that <u>ye stand on the brink of destruction</u>! And for that do we thy Brothers reach out that ye may not be destroyed -- So be it and Selah -- Now it is given unto me to come unto thee and I shall give unto thee as ye are prepared to receive - for it is the better part of wisdom that ye are prepared --

So be it and Selah – Now ye shall give unto thy Benefactors credit for knowing that which they say unto thee - and ye shall be wise to heed that which they say -- So be it and Selah -- I now give unto thee my word that ye shall be delivered out before the "great and terrible day" - all which are so prepared - and ye shall know no sorrow -- So be it and Selah -- I am thy Brother Bor ---

* * *

Beloved of my being: Ye shall now give unto them the words of our beloved Sister of Light - Bere - for she has not spoken unto them before. Now she shall break the silence and it shall serve to prepare them for the part which she has kept for them -- So be it and Selah -- I am Sananda ---

Bere

Beloved children of Earth: Be ye blest of my presence - for I too come unto thee out of the Inner Temple - and I shall give unto thee that which I have prepared for thee -- For ye shall come to know me as one of thy Benefactors - for I have given unto thee of myself that ye may come into the fullness of thy inheritance -- So be it and Selah -- Now ye have asked for more light and for that do I now come unto thee -- For it is given unto me to be one sent out from the Father that ye may come to know thy oneness with all things --

And thy Brothers of Light have volunteered to give unto thee of themselves - of their love - their grace - their mercy and wisdom that ye may know as they know - that ye may return unto the Father - the Source of thy being -- So be it and Selah -- Are ye not mindful of them wherein ye have been comforted and provided for - wherein ye have found succor in time of sorrow and wherein ye shall be rescued -- Wherein is it said that they have come that ye may be delivered? So be it and Selah -- I am one which shall stand ready to answer thy call - so be it in love wisdom and prudence -- I am thy Sister of the Inner Temple. Bere ---

* * *

Part #59

Beloved of my being: Now ye shall add unto these that of blessed Brother of Light - Boran - and it shall serve to give them more light -- So be it and Selah -- I am Sananda ---

Boran

Beloved of my being: Be ye as one which has my hand upon thee and ye shall be blest as I have been blest of the Father -- So be it and Selah -- I am thy Sibor and I have so prepared thee -- So be it and Selah -- Now ye shall give unto them as I shall give unto thee - and ye shall be unto them that which I shall be unto thee -- So be it in the name of the Most High Living God -- Now ye shall send unto them these words which ye shall record for them:

Beloved of my being: Be ye as ones which have my hand upon thee and I shall bless them as I have been blest -- So be it and Selah -- I say unto thee as have my beloved Brothers - that many stand ready to come unto thee - and to give unto thee that which they have received of the Father for thee --

For it is the day of the "New Dispensation" wherein ye shall have thy freedom - and ye have but to claim it in the name of the Father - Son and Holy Ghost -- So be it and Selah -- Now ye shall be told many things which have hitherto been held secret - and ye shall be as ones awakened from a deep yet troubled sleep - and ye shall be glad for thy awakening ---

And for that do I now come unto thee that ye may awaken -- And I shall give unto thee that which shall serve to awaken thee and ye shall be glad forevermore - for ye shall go into darkness no more - and ye shall stand free in the light of the Christ made whole -- So be it and Selah -- I am one which has given of myself that ye may have thy freedom --So be it and Selah -- I am thy Older Brother from out of the Inner Temple - Boran ---

* * *

Soran

Beloved of my being: Ye shall now receive that which I have kept for thee and ye shall give it unto them -- For it is now come when they shall have the part which has been kept for this time -- I am one which has prepared them that they may be prepared to receive the "greater part". So be it and Selah -- I am thy Brother Soran --

Beloved ones which are within the places wherein ye labor for bread: Have ye not been in darkness and despair - have ye not given unto the forces of darkness thy strength - and thy time? Have ye not wearied of the darkness - and shall ye not be delivered out? Wherein have ye sought thy freedom - and wherein have ye known freedom?

Now it is come when ye shall be delivered and when ye shall come to know freedom as ye have not known it --

And for that do I now come unto thee that ye may be delivered -- For it is given unto me to be free and I can speak with authority -- And it is given unto me to know the law and to be one with it - and now I come unto thee that ye may know and that ye may receive as I have received -- So be it and Selah -- Now I shall give unto thee that which ye are prepared to receive and no more -- For it is the better part of wisdom that ye consume that which ye have been given -- And yet for them which are prepared to receive the "greater part" - they shall be plucked from out of the "world of men" and they shall be prepared for the great initiation which shall be unto them their inheritance.

They shall be freed from all bondage - all limitations - and they shall go into the Temple of the Most High Living God - and therein they shall receive of the Father that which He has willed unto them -- And they shall become as He and they shall be given the power and the authority to create as He creates - in His likeness and in His image and they shall go into darkness no more --

So be it every man's inheritance - and he shall be as one reborn - and as one illumined - and I shall return into the "world of men" as the emissary of the Father -- For that have many been prepared and many have come into the Earth from three different planets within the solar system that this may be accomplished -- For it is the New Age when ye shall come to know them which have given of themselves that this may be brot about ---

I am one which has worked for many ages that the Earth and Her inhabitants may be illumined - for sad indeed are the ones in darkness.

Now it is come when the darkness shall be dispelled from the Earth and She shall become a shining orb within the solar system -- Now I say unto thee that ye shall come to know that which has hitherto been kept secret -- Ye shall be true unto thyself - for ye shall not deceive thyself.

For the Father nor thy Sibors and Benefactors are not deceived - for as ye are prepared so shall ye receive - and none other shall partake of this secret doctrine and its wisdom - For eons of time has it been protected from the infamous and the profane -- Now again we the guardians of these secrets have opened the way that they which have prepared themselves and have received of the Sibors may be prepared may enter into the chambers of the Most High Living God -- So be it and Selah -- Now I am one who stands guard at the gate that none other pass save they who are prepared -- And as ye are prepared ye shall be brot into the outer temple and prepared for the inner -- So be it and Selah -- I am thy Sibor and older Brother - Soran ---

(The Beloved Soran and Moraya are one and the same.)

* * *

Berean

Beloved of my being: Be ye as one which has my hand upon thee and ye shall receive of me - and ye shall come into the place wherein I am as one prepared -- So be it and Selah -- Now ye shall give unto them this portion which I have prepared for them -- So be it that it shall serve them well ---

Beloved children which are yet in darkness: Be ye as one which has my hand upon thee and I shall bless thee as I have been blest -- So be it and Selah -- I am come unto thee that ye may be blest - that ye may receive as I have received of the Father -- So be it and Selah -- I am one of the Eloheim and I have been given the power and the authority of the Father - and He has invested within me the Love and Wisdom which is His --

And now He has opened the way that ye too shall receive as I have received - and for that have I now revealed myself unto thee -- So be it that I shall come unto thee and I shall sibor thee as ye are prepared to receive me -- So be it in love - wisdom and prudence -- For I know wherein ye are - and wherein ye are prepared -- So be it and Selah -- Be ye of a mind to comprehend that which I say unto thee - for it shall be thy passport into the secret place of the Most High ---

Now again I shall give unto thee the key for thy deliverance - and ye shall use it and it shall become part of thy being - and it shall be unto thee thy freedom from bondage: "Father - Thy Will be done in me - thru me - by me - and for me"-- So be it and Selah -- I am one which has awaited this day when I might come unto thee and sibor thee and give unto thee as I have received --

So be it is now come - and I shall stand ready to come unto thee and sibor thee in the laws of the Losoloes wherein ye shall come to master all that ye survey in love - wisdom - and prudence - wherein ye shall know the law of thy Oneness - the law of thy Being -- So be it and Selah. I am thy Older Brother - Berean ---

Beloved ones which are yet in darkness: I come unto thee from out of the Temple of Light that ye may have more light -- I bring unto thee a plan which has been fashioned to deliver thee from thy bondage of darkness forever -- For it has been given unto thee to stumble in darkness for long -- Now ye are offered a plan which shall bring thee out and ye shall return unto the Father and be made whole -- So be it and Selah -- Now ye shall ask and ye shall seek and apply thyself wholeheartedly that ye may be prepared to partake of this plan and to receive the fruits thereof --

For it is the law and that which none may break -- So be it and Selah Now I say unto thee that ye have gone thru the valley of darkness for the last time - for it is now come when each and every one shall be brot out of the Earth and ye shall come to know the depth of darkness wherein ye have been -- So be it and Selah -- I am thy Older Brother and Sibor - Berean ---

* * *

Sananda

Beloved: Ye shall add this unto the others - for it shall be given unto them as one part -- For it is the better part of wisdom that they come to know their Benefactors -- For as one shall sibor one sibet in one part of the law - another shall take the responsibility for another sibet and another part of the law --

And they shall rotate until they have completed their instruction in the laws of the Losoloes -- So be it that they shall know as the Sibors and as the Father which has formulated the plan and given unto us of Himself that we may become as He is -- So be it and Selah -- And now I say unto them that it is the better part of wisdom to be prepared to receive of thy Benefactors - so shall it serve thee well -- I am thy Sibor and thy Brother - Sananda ---

Recorded by Sister Thedra

Part #60

Beloved of my being: Be ye as one which has my hand in thine - and I shall lead thee out of the place wherein ye are - and ye shall come into the place wherein I am as one prepared -- So be it and Selah -- Now ye shall give unto them that which shall be given unto them - that which shall be given unto thee for them by our beloved Brother which has gone the Royal Road - Bernard - so shall it profit them - Sananda

Bernard

Beloved Sister of the Emerald Cross: Be ye as one which has my hand upon thee and ye shall receive as I have received -- So be it and Selah I am come unto thee that ye may receive for them the part which I have prepared for them -- So be it and Selah ---

Beloved ones which have asked for more light: I say unto thee that it is now offered unto thee and ye have but to accept it - and ye shall be prepared for that -- For now it is come when ye shall move out of thy present place into the place wherein is much light -- It is not lawful to give unto thee that which ye are not prepared to receive

Yet ye shall receive as ye are prepared -- Now ye shall come to know the wisdom of that statement for that is a part which shall be given unto thee - and ye shall abide by the law ---

Now ye have asked for more light - and many shall reach out that ye shall find thy way - and ye shall be mindful of them - for they shall be sent unto thee and they shall be unto thee all that ye shall need -- For it is given unto them to know thee - and to know thy needs and to supply them --

Now ye shall put from thee all fear and hatred - all which is not like unto the Christ - and ye shall ask of the Father that ye may receive thy freedom thru Him -- And ye shall be sent one which shall bring thee that which the Father shall give them for thee - so shall it serve thee well -- I am thy Sibor and thy Brother - Bernard --

Sananda

Beloved of my being: Be ye as one which has my hand upon thee and ye shall receive of me as I have received -- So be it and Selah -- Now ye shall give unto them that which I shall give unto thee for them - so shall they come to know them which stand ready to serve them in the light of the Christ -- So be it and Selah -- I am thy Sibor and I have prepared thee that ye may receive as I have received -- So be it and Selah -- I Am Sananda ---

Beloved one which I call my own: It is now come when ye shall come into the place wherein I am and ye shall receive of me as I have received of the Father - and ye shall be glad forevermore -- Now I have given unto thee much which is designed to awaken thee - and yet ye are in a state of Lethargy –

Ye have not stirred thyself - and ye shall have cause to remember that which has been said unto thee -- for it is now come when ye shall be brot out of the Earth - and ye shall be put into a place which ye are prepared for - for ye have given little thot unto that which has been said unto thee and less unto thy preparation -- So be it that ye shall be caught up short and ye shall cry Lord! Lord! and ye shall be as one bound in darkness and ye shall have no peace --

For it is come when thy science shall fail to comfort thee and ye shall have no place to lay thy head -- Ye shall be as foxes without burrows - so shall it be -- And ye have been told time and again that it is the better part of wisdom to prepare thyself that ye may be delivered before that "great terrible day"- yet ye are as one with feet of lead and ye have fallen into thy lethargy time after time -- So be it and alas! - ye shall remember these words for they shall ring in thy ears and ye shall cry out for help - yet ye shall be as one which has thrown thy life belt overboard -- So be it that I now say unto thee again - to alert thyself and be about thy salvation and ye shall know no sorrow or suffering -- So be it and Selah -- I am thy Sibor and thy Brother - Sananda ---

Recorded by Sister Thedra

Mission Statement

Give the truth to the world. Let it be received where it will. Many will read the messages. Some will accept the truth, others will read through curiosity, a few will ridicule. Yet to all is the truth given, and to all remains the power of choice.

The hope of the world in these times is in spiritualizing all forms of activity---promoting understanding through love and service. These must be the watchwords if the world is to come into lasting peace. We are trying to influence a world that is going astray and could cause undreamed of suffering. We are trying to overcome the thought of materialists and to bring a spiritual outlook into the earthly life. We need the help of all on earth who can think in spiritual terms. The great battle to be fought now is between the spiritual and the material, between idealism and carnalism. You can help by spreading the word---we are asking that you help because the battle may be long and the victory far away.

Halls of Light is not allied with any sect, denomination, political entity, organization, neither endorses nor opposes any cause. There are no dues for membership. Halls of Light is self-supporting through its own voluntary contributions. Halls of Light has but one purpose: to help through encouragement and understanding...

To contact the publishers or to obtain copies of our other books, please contact us at email: goldtown11@gmail.com

Sananda's Appearance

Be ye as one which hast heard Mine Voice and responded unto it - for I speak that ye hear, and I say that which is wise and prudent.

Let it be known that 1, the Lord thy God hast spoken and bear ye witness of Me, for I have made manifest Mineself that ye might know Me - and for this wast these manifestations made.

I say that I have made Mineself manifest that ye might see Me with thine mortal eyes; that ye might bear witness of Me. Yet thine companions saw and believed not; neither did they hear, for they were selfish and unprepared - yet, did I deny them?

I say; I came that they which would might see and hear. I went and came again unto Mine own. So be it that I have found; I have given unto the found that they which know not might know; that they might come to know as thou knowest.

Yet, how many hast turned from Me and persecuted thee for Mine Word. It is said, "Woe unto them which persecute Mine servants." is it not the law which they set into motion?

Yea Mine beloved, I say they bring about their own downfall. So be it that I am a compassionate one, and I would that they know what they do. So be it they shall learn well their lessons. So let it be, for this is the mercy of God, the One which hast sent Me.

So be it. I AM The Wayshower, the Lord thy God

I AM Sananda

Authority to Use the Name Sananda

Sori Sori: Mine hand I have placed upon thine head, and I have given unto thee the authority to use Mine name. For I first showed Mineself unto thee with the Word: "Go feed Mine sheep. Give unto them the name Sananda, by which they shall know Me as the Lord thy God - the Son of God sent that ye be made to know Me - the One sent from out the Inner Temple that there be Light in the world of men."

Now it is come when ones which have the will to follow Me shall come to know Me by that name which I commanded thee to give unto the world as Mine "New Name." There are many which shall call upon the name of Jesus, yet they will deny the New Name as they are want to do. While unto thee I give assurance that I am the One sent that there be Light in the world of men. Now let this be understood, that they which deny Mine New Name deny Me by any name. So be it I have appointed thee Mine spokesman; I've given unto thee the power and authority to speak for being that which I AM. And I say unto thee Mine child whom I have called forth and anointed thee with the Holy Spirit, thy name shall be as it is now called, Thedra - that name I spoke unto thee from out the eth, and thou heard Me and accepted that which I gave unto thee; and wherein have I deceived thee? Wherein have i forgotten thee, or left thee alone?

I say unto thee, Mine hand is upon thee and I shall sustain thee and ye shall come to know that which I have kept for thee. So be it that I have kept thy reward, and at no time shall it be dissipated or scattered, for it is intact. So let this Mine Word suffice them which question thee - let them question, and I shall bear witness for thee. For do I not know Mine servants from the traitor? Do I not reward Mine servants according unto their works or merits? I speak that they might know that I am mindful of mine servants, that I am not a poor puny priest who hast forgotten his servants.

I say unto them, Mine servants shall be glorified above the crowned heads of the nations which have set themselves apart, and denied Me Mine part of Mine Word - for they have turned from Me in their conceit and forgetfulness.

Now let this go on record as Mine Word, and I shall give unto them proof, which are of a mind to follow Me. So be it I have spoken and I am not finished; I shall speak again and again, and I shall raise Mine Voice against them which set foot against Mine servants, and they shall be as ones cast out. So let them ask of Me and I shall enlighten them. So be it I know whereof I speak. Be ye as ones blest to accept Me and know Me for that which I AM.

Sananda

About the Late Sister Thedra

Since the later part of the last Century the Kumara wisdom preserved by Aramu Muru has begun to reemerge into the world. This process began with the late Sister Thedra, whom Jesus Christ appeared physically to while on her deathbed and spontaneously healed her of cancer while she was in the Yucatan, where she had gone to accept her fate, and the will of our Lord Jesus Christ.

That is when something miraculous occurred. Jesus spoke to her saying, "My name is Esu Sananda Kumara" and then sent Thedra down to the Monastery of the Seven Rays to learn the Kumara wisdom. After five years, Thedra was told to return to the United States where she founded the Association of Sananda and Sanat Kumara at Mt. Shasta in California.

While heading this organization, Thedra channeled many messages from Sananda and taught the Kumara wisdom until her passing in 1992. While in the Yucatan it is said that while Sister during the 1960s Thedra was in the Yucatan, she was told a secret by her friend George Hunt Williamson, also known as Brother Philip, who authored Secrets of the Andes, and the SECRET PLACES OF THE LION.

Williamson, confided in his long-time friend Sister Thedra that he intentionally scrambled the reincarnational lineages in order to protect this next generation when they the Mayan Solar Priests, who were the direct line descendants of the Kumara according to prophesy were scheduled to reincarnate or return to fulfill their missions upon Earth, one of which was to relocate these ancient sites where the original records of the Amaru were placed for safe keeping.

Sister Thedra, 1900-1992, spent five years at the abbey undergoing intensive spiritual training and initiations. While in South America in the Yucatan, she had an experience which changed her in an instant when as it is told by her that Jesus Christ physically appeared to her and spontaneously cured her of cancer.

He introduced himself to her by his true, name, "Sananda Kumara," thereby revealing his affiliation with the Venusian founders of the Great Solar Brotherhoods. It was by his command that Sister Thedra went to Peru where in here travels she met Williamson.

Sister Thedra eventually left Peru upon telling her experience there was complete. Even before she returned to the States she met with harsh criticism from the church, which she elected to leave. She then traveled to Mt. Shasta in California and founded the Association of Sananda and Sanat Kumara. A.S.S.K.

You ask, Is There A Difference Between Jesus and Sananda? Our Lords name given at birth by his Father Joseph, and his beloved mother Mary was Yeshua, thus being of the house of David and the order of Yoseph, he would be called Yeshua ben Yoseph. The Roman Emperors placed the name of Jesus upon the sir name of Yeshua, after the Emperor Justinian adopted Christianity as the official faith of Rome, and ordered that the sacred books be compiled, upon approval of a specially appointed council, appointed by the Emperor, into a recognizable and uniform work titled The Bible. Prior to this there never was a Bible per se.

There existed until the time of the Emperor's edict, a selection of many Sacred texts, that were employed in the Sacred Teachings. Many of which were copies of what the Greeks had transposed from the original texts in the Libraries of Alexandria, which were originally compiled by Alexander the Great, and were destroyed by Julius Caesar, fearing that they might prove dangerous to the rule of a Caesar, an Earthly God.

In addition, it kept. (he thought) the knowledge of Alexander's Libraries, out of the hands of the Ptolemy's, who were said to be descended from his bloodline. At the time Caesar had no way of knowing the vast portions of the Library that were already in the Americas, in the Great Universities of the Inca, and the Maya. Yeshua spent many years in the East after his ascension. The good Sheppard, upon his appearances to the Apostles after his ascension told his Apostles that he was in fact going to tend to his Father's other sheep; which means, plainly that he was continuing upon his sacred journey. As the ascended one, Yeshua took to himself the name of Sananda, meaning the Christed one, and Sananda was thus embraced forever more by the Great Solar Brotherhood. To many of you this is all new, to others it will be received as a welcome easing of the wall that has so long separated two sides of the same coin, this is being placed into the ethers and the matrix of thought at this time as it is the time of the Awakening, and the Christos is already emerging into the new consciousness, and mother Earth herself. Sister Thedra and the phenomenon of channeling.

Authority to use the name of Sananda was given to Sister Thedra when Jesus~ Sananda appeared to her in the Yucatan, and cured her instantly of the cancer that had taken her body over. Further, he allowed a picture of his countenance to be taken at that time that she might realize the occurrence was more than a dream. Thedra had a large format camera called a 620 and it had bellows on it and founded out. She used this to take the picture of Sananda.

Sanada's Message to her by Sister Thedra. "Sori Sori: Mine hand I have placed upon thine head, and I have given unto thee the authority to use Mine name. Give unto them the name Sananda, by which they shall know Me as the Lord thy God - the Son of God, sent that ye be made to know me, the One sent from out the inner temple that there be Light in the world of men." Now it is come when ones which have the will to follow Me shall come to know Me by that name which I commanded thee to give unto the world as Mine "New name."

There are many that shall call upon the name of Jesus, yet, they will deny the new name as they are want to do. While unto thee I give assurance that I am the One sent that there be Light in the world of men. Now let this be understood, that they that deny Mine New Name deny Me by any name. So be it I have appointed thee Mine spokesman; I've given unto thee the power and authority to speak for being that which I AM. And I say unto thee Mine child whom I have called forth and anointed thee with the Holy Spirit, thy name shall be as it is now called, Thedra - that name I spoke unto thee from out the ethers, and thou heard Me and accepted that which I gave unto thee; and wherein have I deceived thee? Wherein have I forgotten thee, or left thee alone?"

"I say unto thee, Mine hand is upon thee and I shall sustain thee and you shall come to know that which I have kept for thee. So be it that I have kept thy reward, and at no time shall it be dissipated of scattered, for it is intact. So let this Mine Word suffice them which question thee - let them question, and I shall bear witness for thee. For do I not know Mine servants from the traitor? Do I not reward Mine servants according unto their works or merits? I speak that they might know that I am mindful of Mine servants, that I am not a poor puny priest who has forgotten his servants."

"I say unto them, Mine servants shall be glorified above the crowned heads of the nations which have set themselves apart, and denied Me Mine part of Mine word for they have turned from Me in their conceit and forgetfulness." "Now let this go on record as Mine Word, and I shall give unto them proof, which are of a mind to follow Me. So be it as I have spoken and I am not finished; I shall speak again and again, and I shall rise Mine Voice against them which set foot against Mine servants, and they shall be as ones cast out. So let them ask of Me and I shall enlighten them. So be it I know where of I speak. Be ye as ones blest to accept Me and know Me for that which I AM. The Final Messages on Saturday, June 13, 1992, at exactly 10.00 PM, at the age of 92, Sister Thedra made her final transition from the comfort of her own bed. When the time arrived, she simply took one small breath and slipped quietly away, without pomp or fanfare.

She left as she had lived...as a humble servant for the greater good. The messages that follow were given to Sister Thedra shortly before her transition. They are compiled here to give you some idea of the significance of her passing and of the expansion of the work, as she is now free to work unencumbered by the physical limitations and by the pain which has so encumbered her in the past. She has carried on the work here on the Earth plane for the last 50 years because that's where the work was needed...rest assured that her work now in the higher realms will simply be an extension of that work.

www.ingramcontent.com/pod-product-compliance
Lightning Source LLC
LaVergne TN
LVHW051516070426
835507LV00023B/3141